CU00821996

The V**oi**ce of Leadership

Six Keys to *Presence*
Influence, and
Creative *Confidence*

SALLY MABELLE

The Voice of Leadership: Six Keys to Presence, Influence, and Creative Confidence

First published by Hetherington, Heinbach, and Hall

Tāmaki Makaurau / Auckland City, New Zealand 1010

Copyright © 2017 by Sally Mabelle.

All rights reserved.

No part of this book may be reproduced, stored in a retrieval system, or transmitted by any means without the written permission of the author.

Sally Mabelle
+6421 0222 8782
sally@sallymabelle.com
www.sallymabelle.com

ISBN: (sc) 978-0-473-40020-0

Printed in Tāmaki Makaurau, Aotearoa
New Zealand by Bookprinting.co.nz

Dedication

To the One Spirit that dwells within all.
May this book serve the reader to heed Its call.

Mihi

Acknowledgements

He toa takitini tāku toa
ehara it te toa takitahi.

My courage is the courage of many, not just mine alone.
Traditional Māori whakataukī (proverb)

I have been blessed with many mentors and teachers on the path to writing this book. Firstly, thank you (ngā mihi[1]) to my mother, Margaret Ann Heinbach. You have passed on your spontaneity, humour, playfulness, passionate expressiveness and enjoyment of life's simple pleasures. Ngā mihi to my father, Richard Graham

Williams, who passed on a sense of responsibility, discipline, and his deeply held values which he quietly embodied. Ngā mihi to my main life cheerleaders, my partner, David Dominko Hrstich and my adopted 'mum,' Joyce Hrstich. You have been my closest supporters for the past 14 years. When I lost my trust, you helped me find it again. Ngā mihi to the organisations which hired me to inspire and educate your people. You have helped me live out my mission: New Zealand Trade and Enterprise, University of Auckland, Auckland University of Technology (AUT), J. Walter Thompson, Westpac Bank, AMP, Minter Ellison Rudd Watts, New Zealand Business Excellence Foundation (NZBEF), Drake International, Spotless Services, New Zealand Fire Service, YMCA, YWCA, ANZIIF, Landcare Research, Auckland City Council, KPMG, NZ Ministry of Education, James and Wells, Achieve Global, Zealmark Group, TEDx speakers, Aquarium and Zoo Association (Australia and New Zealand), SIFA, AAPNZ, Toastmasters NZ, NZSDT, FINZ, St. Mary's College, Duet Productions, Pennsylvania Trust Company, Johnson and Johnson Pharmaceuticals, HMO-PA/NJ, Roach Brothers Realtors, John Casablancas Talent Agency, and so on.

To my wise woman friends and confidantes, Anna Cowan, Janey Hunter, Joan Levy, Priya McCulloch, Thomas Huffman, and Diana Coia, ngā mihi for your love, unconditional acceptance, encouragement, and belief in me and my work. To my singing and acting teachers: Janis Dardaris, Gordon Phillips, Michael Deason-Barrow, Carolyn Val-Schmidt, Divvy Nelson, Rosina Gore, Rajeswar Bhattacharya, Sharmila Banerjee, Jill Purce, Gilles Petit, and Chris James, ngā mihi for generously sharing your creative talents. Ngā mihi to my colleagues at the National Speakers' Association of New Zealand (NSANZ) and to my NSA-Australia colleagues for your support and professional acknowledgement. Ngā mihi for my publishing team for their support and attention to detail in birthing this book: To Sue Reidy and Rebecca McIntyre for initial manuscript assessments, to Suzanne Hardy for meticulous proofreading and patience, to Eva Brichau for her positive attitude and willing flexibility in persisting to get the book design just right, to Arthur Angelo for his creativity and exemplary customer service in designing the book cover, and to my beloved and talented son, Orion Mabelle, for his artistic illustrations. Ngā mihi to my te reo Māori tutors at Unitec for generously sharing your wisdom, knowledge, and love of the Māori language and culture: Kiri Neho, Tuatahi Pene, and Joe Naden. Ngā mihi to all my mentoring clients who confided in me and allowed me to do what I love in supporting you to be your best.

Preface

The Early Days

I was seven years old and swinging on my backyard swingset. My three sisters were on the swings next to me. We were all pumping our little legs and arms to see who could swing the highest. At the same time, our father was watching us and singing the old Broadway tunes that he loved. We were all singing along with him at the top of our lungs and on the last line of each song, we would launch off our swings to see who could jump out the farthest. Being the oldest, I usually won.

The Teenage Years

It was not until I was a teenager that my sisters would start beating me in our games. Our high school lacrosse coach shouted at me as we ran wind sprints, "Hurry up, Williams, you're not going to let your little sister beat you, are you?" I was neck and neck with my sister, horrified and shamed when she finished first.

My next youngest sister started surpassing me in another arena. She won all the lead roles in our high school plays and always got to sing the lead part in our church choir. I remember my heart sinking when my father was listening to us practise a duet to sing at our friend's wedding. Dad said, "Sally, let your sister sing the high notes. You stick with the low notes." I felt crushed. I was the oldest and my little sisters were leaving me in the dust. Oh, the shame!

Early Career Years

It was not until I graduated from university and moved to San Francisco to work for a software company that I stopped comparing myself to my sisters to start down my own path. By the time I was 25 years old, my creativity was smoldering under my corporate business suit. I grew restless with my job of coordinating the design, installation, and debugging of financial software systems. I longed for more creative self-expression. I ended up enrolling in Tony Buzan's Mind Mapping course and teaching this new creativity tool to my team. Shortly afterwards, I attended an evening acting course which lit up a new passion for me. I summoned up the courage to make the leap. To the surprise and alarm of my parents and my manager, I announced that I was leaving the company to pursue a career in acting.

Professional Acting to Personal Development

For three years I waited tables and drove a pizza delivery truck while I acted in every commercial, musical theatre, and play I could find. I also taught voice and acting at a talent agency. Life then led me sideways, as it often does, to a personal growth seminar called 'Insight I.' This experience was so powerful I was inspired to change course once again, and I became a personal and professional development facilitator, teaching leadership development courses while immersing myself in a Spiritual Psychology master's degree programme for the next few years. It was during that programme when I met my then husband who persuaded me to move with him to Boulder, Colorado (the 'most conscious city in the U.S.A.' as he described it).

In Boulder, I launched my 'Life Design Consulting' business and gave my first 'Speak with Power, Poise, and Presence' presentation to around 100 executives at the Boulder Chamber of Commerce. Helping others to express themselves and their authentic voice has been my passion ever since.

I have spent the past 25 years developing the 'Voice of Leadership' method of building executive presence, influence and creative confidence. In my journey to find and express my own authentic voice of leadership, as an executive mentor, facilitator, trainer, and speaker, I have discovered many proven and practical techniques which I have collated and condensed to share here with you. My path has been filled with many successes and equally just as many failures, flops, and embarrassing moments I would rather forget.

Success is stumbling from failure to failure with no loss of enthusiasm.

Winston Churchill

It is my wish to save you precious time and to fast track your progress to fully owning and expressing your voice of leadership. I have worked with leaders in many professional service organisations such as the IT, banking, insurance, accounting, and healthcare industries. I have also worked with not-for-profits and a variety of schools in the U.S.A. and New Zealand. My educational and professional background encompasses a number of fields including rhetoric and communication, education, psychology and acting. I have integrated lessons from all these areas and organised them into six keys for Voice of Leadership development. Think of me as your guide and companion on your personal and professional development journey.

An Introduction Aotearoa (New Zealand Māori) Style:

In Aotearoa, New Zealand, the place I now call home, the indigenous Māori way of introducing oneself is via a pepeha; a brief presentation beginning with one's homeland and ancestry. In te ao Māori (the Māori world), family ties are deeply respected and honoured. Since moving from the U.S.A. to Aotearoa, New Zealand 14 years ago and studying te reo Māori (the Māori language), I have developed a greater appreciation for the significance of my whakapapa (lineage) as a treasured gift (tāonga tuku īho) being handed down to future generations (ngā iwi āpōpō). In my pepeha below, I honour my roots and lineage, including the Native American Lenape tribe of my homeland (followed by the English translation).

Ko Wissahickon ko Delaware ko Schuylkill ngā awa.
Ko Kitahikàn Atlantic te moana.
Ko Wēra, Ko Kōterana, Ko Ingarani, Ko Tiamana ōku hanga whakapapa.
Ko Armstrong, Ko Bell, Ko Durborough, Ko Graham, Ko Hall, Ko Harrison, Ko Heinbach, Ko Hetherington, Ko Jones, Ko Mason, Ko Richardson, Ko Spencer, Ko Thomas, Ko Wharton, Ko Warwick, Ko Williams ōku whanau whanui.
No Blue Bell, Nitapekunk Philadelphia, Pennsylvania ahau.

Kei Tāmaki Makaurau, Aotearoa ahau e noho ana.

Hei kaiārahi o te waha o te mana tāku mahi,

Ko Sally Mabelle tōku ingoa.

Kia ora mai tatou.[1]

The Wissahickon, the Delaware, and the Schuylkill are my rivers.

The Atlantic is my ocean.

My ancestors are from Wales, Scotland, England and Germany.

My extended family surnames are Armstrong, Bell, Durborough, Graham, Hall, Harrison, Heinbach, Hetherington, Jones, Mason, Richardson, Spencer, Thomas, Warwick, Wharton, and Williams.

I come from Blue Bell, Philadelphia, Pennsylvania.

I now live in Auckland, New Zealand.

I am a mentor in the voice of leadership.

My name is Sally Mabelle.

Greetings to all.

Contents

Introduction

Congratulations! Whether you are an executive, an aspiring leader, an entrepreneur, a job seeker, a career changer, a mentor, or a coach, you have just discovered a unique resource for your personal and professional development. From my own experience, through many trials and errors as well as through extensive research, I have collated many of my favourite tried and true resources for your empowerment. This book is filled with stories, insights, and practical tips to boost your 'voice of leadership.'

What is the Voice of Leadership and how can it Help You?

The 'voice of leadership' is an umbrella term I use to group some of the key, yet sometimes overlooked ingredients which go into the making of positive, powerful and influential leaders. Combined, these ingredients can develop you into someone who is engaging and creative, with a strong voice and presence; clear, confident, and connected to your highest aspirations and purpose. Whether or not you actually have a designated leadership position in an organisation, you will benefit from developing your leadership qualities and capacities. Today, with the ease of connecting and communicating with anyone in the world via the internet and modern technologies, the old style of top down, hierarchical leadership is giving way to a more collaborative style. In this new era you have the opportunity to be more influential and connected with a greater number of people than ever before. It is no longer appropriate to rely on one specific leader to show the way. All of us can develop our leadership potential within our own unique sphere of influence.

The voice of leadership can help you gain a promotion, make a sale, or lead your team and/or organisation through the change process. Whether you want to more powerfully present yourself at team meetings, board meetings, and interviews, or to more clearly develop and present proposals or confront challenging situations like performance reviews, this book provides practical tools for you to develop your leadership presence. Essentially, anyone who wants to develop their executive presence, influence and creative confidence will benefit from the information in this book.

With sustained focus on the key themes in this book, you will:

- elevate your personal brand

- increase your ability to own the room and to act with intent and purpose

- build your resilience and composure in challenging situations

- improve your ability to engage others with an authentic 'voice of authority'

- build trust in your own ideas and creativity

- be better able to inspire others to align with your vision or projects

- be better able to collaborate and resolve any interpersonal conflicts

In an increasingly interconnected and overstimulating world, your voice of leadership will differentiate you and help you to stand out from the crowd. This book is your toolkit of critical insights, powerful exercises, and new skills.

Your Voice of Leadership Self-Assessment Tool

To help you gauge your progress I recommend you complete the 'voice of leadership' online self-assessment tool before reading Chapter 1. This tool will increase your awareness of your strengths and challenges as regards presence, influence and creative confidence. Once you have read the book and practised some of the tools for a minimum recommended period of 12 weeks or more, take the self-assessment again. You should see your self-rating rise significantly. You can find the self-assessment tool by scrolling down the home page at www.sallymabelle.com. If you prefer to practise with others and would like the social support and accountability of a group mentoring experience, you can find out more about opportunities for you to participate online and in person by signing up to my newsletter at – www.sallymabelle.com/contact-us.

The Six Keys to your Voice of Leadership

Each of the voice of leadership keys is accompanied by practical exercises. We will focus on developing your voice and vision, vitality, values, visibility, and veneration (influential, respectful communication). When you are operating skilfully in each of these six areas, you will be well-prepared to have maximum impact and to make your greatest contribution in both your personal and professional life.

A Growth Mindset Approach

I suggest that you approach the information in this book with what is known as a 'growth mindset.' Stanford University psychologist, Carol Dweck,[1] who pioneered the idea of mind-sets, says that people with a growth mindset embrace change and challenges. If you adopt the attitude that you will become more capable and knowledgeable, even if you make some mistakes along the way, you will be more successful in developing your voice of leadership. Be willing to engage with the ideas and exercises presented here, to find out for yourself, through the feedback and results you get, what works best for you.

To boost your self-awareness even further, take a look at the Voice of Leadership Virtuosity Scale below. The six keys are shown on a continuum from 1 to 7. Circle the number which best fits your current level of mastery in each area.

If you give yourself a low rating on any of the keys, you may want to pay extra attention to those areas as you progress through the book.

The Voice of Leadership Virtuosity Scale

Circle the number on the scale to indicate your current level of virtuosity:

Key #1 Voice

Powerless   Powerful
    1   2   3   4   5   6   7

Key #2 Vision

Stagnant   Creative
    1   2   3   4   5   6   7

Key #3 Vitality

Apathetic   Enthusiastic
    1   2   3   4   5   6   7

Key #4 Values

Incongruent   Integrated
    1   2   3   4   5   6   7

Key #5 Visibility

Invisible   Visible
    1   2   3   4   5   6   7

Key #6 Veneration

Insensitive   Respectful
    1   2   3   4   5   6   7

Think of the voice of leadership as a whole circle or wheel. To give you a visual picture of where your wheel may need a rebalancing and an alignment, see the Voice of Leadership Wheel below.

The Voice of Leadership Wheel

1. Draw a line across the centre of each section to indicate where you currently rate yourself on a scale from 0-10, with 0 at the centre of the circle and 10 on the perimeter of the circle.

2. Connect all the lines to see how balanced your wheel is and where you may need alignment.

3. What action can you take to bring yourself back into balance?

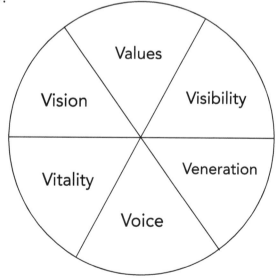

Ideally, you will strive for a balanced level of mastery in all of the key areas, as they are interdependent and integrative. Do you need a voice of leadership wheel alignment? In which of these areas would you like to focus more attention and energy?

How to Use This Book

For maximum effectiveness, I recommend you select a specific time period to focus on intentionally implementing the recommended actions in this book. My clients would normally spend a minimum of 12 weeks and finish their mentoring programme within six months. Pace yourself. You choose the way you want to interact with the book. Achieving a level of mastery in each of the six dimensions will raise you to 'voice of leadership virtuosity.' Are you ready for the challenge? Let us begin.

*Please note that stories throughout this book are based on actual events, however individual client names have been changed throughout to protect privacy.

Voice

What does your voice tell others about you? Like your fingerprint, it reveals your unique identity. Your voice is also an audible barometer broadcasting the pressures you feel in life. Many people experience an unhealthy level of stress which can lead to a constricted voice, impaired creativity and cramped self-expression. We live in a vocally-suppressed society. 'Be quiet', and, 'Be nice' are two phrases you may have heard in one form or another as you grew up. However, you are now wanting to step up and speak out, to express yourself fully and confidently.

Women especially have been suppressed with 'Be quiet', and 'Be nice' messages over the past 5,000 years of recorded history.

It has only been for the last 130 years in Australia and New Zealand, and 96 years in the U.S.A. that women won the right to have their voices count. Prior to that time, women were not expected to have serious opinions worthy of consideration. That means that in the first 97-98% of recorded history women had no public voice. In addition to the pressure to be 'nice', many women face pressures to be thin, to be modest, and to look beautiful. Most men on the other hand, have been programmed from birth that it is not appropriate to show their vulnerability. As a consequence, men have tended to hide their true voice so they will never be seen as weak. This has led many men to suppress their authentic self-expression.

Your Voice and Your Childhood

Did you grow up in an environment that supported you to speak up clearly, boldly, and directly? Were you supported in expressing all your feelings including your anger, sadness, and joy? Any emotional and vocal repression in your childhood will continue to inhibit your voice as an adult unless you become aware of it and commit yourself to overcoming it. With awareness and practise however, you can free yourself from any blocks which hold back your powerful expression.

How did your parents and teachers respond to you when you felt angry? Did you, like some of my clients, get slapped across the face or told that 'children should be seen and not heard'? Did you get a rap across the knuckles or a spanking? Have you ever had your mouth washed out with soap? Or, were you one of the lucky ones instead who was supported in expressing your feelings? If you are like most people, your 'voice of leadership' was suppressed to some extent.

One voice-squelching event happened to me when I was about eight years old. I was standing in the doorway to our kitchen when I must have said something bold and passionate to my mother. She quickly and forcefully grabbed me by the arm, marched me over to the kitchen sink and pushed my head down while she squirted dishwashing liquid into my mouth. I learned in that moment that it was not okay to express myself freely – there may be dangerous consequences! I now understand that my mother was doing what she thought was right at the time. Well-meaning adults who love and support us in many ways can still unintentionally dampen down our voices. As well as forgiving our parents, our challenge is to overcome our voice-suppressing habits and learn how to skillfully express our voice of leadership.

Research Confirms Widespread Vocal Suppression

The late Dr. Stephen R. Covey, well-known leadership teacher and author of the book *Seven Habits of Highly Effective People*[1] cites research in his subsequent book, *The 8th Habit,*[2] which suggests that most people are not speaking up with their voice of leadership. The study which Covey highlights is the Harris Poll, a survey of 23,000 employees completed in 2007. Only 15% of workers reported working in high trust environments and 17% reported having open communication in their organisations. What do these numbers suggest? If people were speaking up clearly, directly, and authentically, the percentage of employees reporting high trust and open communication in their organisations would be much higher.

What Holds You Back?

What is it that keeps you from being fully confident in expressing your voice of leadership? On the top of the list are shame and vulnerability. These subjects have been explored in detail by Dr. Brené Brown, research professor at the University of Houston's College of Social Work. Dr. Brown refers to the inner voice of shame as one which blocks your outer voice. Shame has two messages, says Brown.[3] "Who do you think you are?" and, "You're not good enough!" These two messages are at the core of hesitancy in bold self-expression. Do you recognise these voices? Your habit of toning yourself down to play it safe also puts a damper on your presence, influence, and creative confidence.

The other emotion which may stop you from fully expressing your voice of leadership is the opposite of shame. It is overblown pride or arrogance. Do you ever have a feeling of superiority or disdain in relation to others? Do you ever feel that you are just a bit wiser than other people? Arrogance holds the righteous opinion that you are somehow more worthy of respect than others.

Are you familiar with these two polarities of shame and arrogance? Do you more often have the tendency to view yourself as either superior or inferior? The voice of leadership sweet spot lies somewhere in the middle, grounded in conscious effort and personal humility. In my training as an actor, I discovered one of the ways to find this sweet spot of humble but confident presence was through visualisation. By experimenting with different images, you can learn to embody more presence. Here is a quick experiment for you now:

Presence Visualisation

Imagine yourself as a tree. Stand up and try it now if you are able. Otherwise, sit up tall. Imagine your branches reaching up to the sun and your roots reaching down into the earth. A tree needs to be grounded in the humus (another word for soil, meaning 'earth or ground' in Latin, the root word for humility). A tree also needs the light, yet it can also get burned by the sun (too much sunshine is a metaphor for too much pride which leads to arrogance). Ideally, you come to realise that everyone you interact with is a human being just like you, not better or worse, just different. Stand up or sit up tall at your core – connecting to the earth and also reaching for the sun. Retain a sense of upright, noble posture as you go about your normal activities. Summon the tree image again whenever you want to bolster your presence.

Overcoming the Slippery Snake of Self-Doubt

I personally remember the voice of shame rearing its head when I was asked to enter the New Zealand National Speakers Association (NSANZ) "Inspirational Speaker of the Year" competition. The slippery snake of self-doubt silently hissed, 'Who do you think you are?' and, 'You're not good enough.' I wanted to be liked. I did not want others to think I was being egotistical. I did not apply, as I knew that there were other more experienced speakers who were in my estimation more deserving than I. Only after the prodding of some supportive colleagues did I finally agree to enter the contest. Despite my hesitation to put myself forward, to my delight and surprise, I was ultimately selected by a panel of professional Australian speakers to receive New Zealand's "Inspirational Speaker of the Year" award in 2011. This award served as a strong affirmation and confidence booster for me, especially since the other finalists were all more well-known male speakers. I realised I had been judging them as worthier than myself and that my inner voice of shame was not a reliable authority. One way to overcome self-doubt is to reflect on and recognise the amazing instrument that you have been gifted. Without you doing a thing, your heart is beating, and your lungs are breathing. How is it that all of the trillions of cells in your body are coordinating themselves in harmony without your help? If you have an average heart rate of 60-100 beats per minute (the average range according to Johns Hopkins Medical Centre),[4] that equates to 86,400 to 144,000 heartbeats per day, or 31,536,000 to 52,128,000 heartbeats per year. If you breathe on an average of 12-16 times per minute, that equates to 17,280 to 23,040 breaths per day, or 6,307,200 to

8,409,600 breaths a year. Consider all the billions of cells that are dancing in coordination everyday just to support your life. You are a living, walking miracle!

Glossophobia:

The Common Fear of Public Speaking

It is a common phenomenon to forget about just what an amazing being you are when you are faced with the challenge of public speaking. One of my clients, a CEO working for one of the big four accounting firms, confessed her fear of public speaking to me. She was a well-respected leader and very well-liked, a great networker, yet she had this one last hurdle she could not seem to get over. In her highly visible and influential position, she was being asked to do public speaking more frequently. She had to face the fear and overcome it. As she had endured some painful humiliations in the past, she had developed a tendency to freeze and disassociate from her body whenever she encountered a public speaking situation. The result was that she checked out emotionally and became very robotic when she spoke. By working on practical speech exercises, she was able to transform her anxiety and to strengthen her voice so that she began to actually look forward to and enjoy public speaking. Do you hang back from putting yourself forward when it comes to public speaking or other communication situations that are challenging? It is quite common for even seasoned executives to be fearful of boldly voicing themselves in public. In fact, glossophobia, or the fear of public speaking, is considered the number one fear by many. Executive consultant Dr. Roger Flax surveyed 12,000 senior executives and asked them what their reasons were for being afraid of public speaking.[5] Here are the greatest fears they reported:

- 63% were afraid of being boring

- 71% were afraid of freezing up and forgetting their speech

- 77% were afraid of ruining their career or reputation

- 81% were afraid of making an embarrassing mistake

Fear of Social Rejection

Researchers hypothesise that this intense fear of public speaking is rooted in our evolution. In the past, when human beings were threatened by large predators, living as a group was a critical survival skill. Ostracism or separation of any kind could mean death.[6] No wonder our bodies commonly kick into a stress response when standing up in front of a large group. Standing alone in front of a group of people, no matter what the size, can provoke an intense feeling of separation. On a deep level, we are afraid our audience will reject us. This fear is much greater than the fear of simply being embarrassed or judged. Even stronger is the fear of being rejected from the social group and being left to defend ourselves all alone.

What Confident Speakers Have in Common

It is common knowledge that public speaking nerves can lead to sweaty palms, a pounding heart, a dry mouth and sometimes a struggle to get the right words out. What do confident speakers do to overcome these responses? How can we appear cool and confident? In an analysis of communication samples from TED Speakers, Fortune 500 executives, politicians, and other leaders, researchers identified the key indicators of confidence.[7] Confident speakers exhibit more passion, offer more insight, and are more inclusive. They dig down below the surface of the topics they are presenting and they use more collaborative language to help the audience feel more involved in their message. Words like 'we' and 'let's' for example, indicate a sense of interconnectedness with the audience. It appears that the most confident speakers are community-oriented. By building camaraderie with their listeners, nervous speakers can build confidence and overcome that deep-rooted fear of ostracism. For example, consider some campaign slogans of past popular elections: 'Stronger Together', 'Backing the Kiwi Dream', 'Together, Let's Move Australia Forward' and 'Yes, We Can.

The Impact of Your Voice on Others

Have you ever considered how your voice impacts others? Several Auckland-based law firms have hired me as a mentor for their new partners. They realised the importance of voice in presenting a professional image with clients and colleagues. In one case, a new partner was slurring her words. In another case, the partner's voice was too soft and not assertive enough. In a third case, the issues were colloquial vocabulary and speaking in a monotone. These were all negatively impacting these lawyers' executive presence. Through building awareness and practising simple exercises, they were able to elevate their personal brand, to boost their confidence, and to build trust with their clients and colleagues.

If your voice reflected your authentic power and presence, how would it sound? The Psychological Science Journal published a pioneering study in 2014 which revealed what happens to our voice when placed into circumstances which magnify or diminish our status and power. Researchers found that being put in a position of power can predictably change the way you speak. Voices of individuals placed in high status positions rose in pitch intensity and loudness variability. Listeners use pitch and volume to make accurate inferences about a speaker's hierarchical rank or status. These experiments demonstrate that audible cues are systematically used to reflect and detect status.

Your Multi-Dimensional Voice

There are four interrelated aspects of your voice which affect you and those who listen to you: physical, emotional, mental, and spiritual. Physically, there are certain vocal and breathing techniques which can produce a confident and resonant tone which will boost your sense of authority as well as engage others. Emotionally, your voice reflects your inner feelings as well as your level of warmth and openness. Mentally, your voice contains the thoughts and the structure behind your message. Spiritually, your voice reflects how aligned you are with your highest values and sense of purpose.

I was first introduced to the physical dimensions of voice and speech training when I was in my mid-20s. For several years, I attended master classes at professional theatre schools in acting, voice, and movement in Philadelphia, Pennsylvania. I auditioned for many stage productions, TV commercials, and industrial films and leapt at the opportunity to act both professionally as well as in community productions. As a result, I developed an awareness of the importance of voice as my most powerful communication tool.

One of the major lessons I learned during my years of professional acting was the importance of clear articulation. As actors, we learned that in order to play 'high-status' characters, we need to enunciate concisely and to form our words carefully and intentionally. Only when playing low-status or drunken characters is it appropriate to slur our words. Crisp articulation increases the authority and impact of your speech. As you want to elevate your status to have more presence and influence, practise articulating the way actors do – they often use tongue twisters. These speech exercises require the deliberate and active movement of your tongue, lips, and teeth. Tongue twisters provide an effective way to wake up your speaking agility and clarity. Here are a few I use to warm up with before a presentation or an important meeting. If you visualise yourself speaking to someone who is hard of hearing and needs to read your lips, this will help you put more energy and emphasis into your articulation.

Articulation Exercises (Tongue Twisters)

Red leather, yellow leather (repeat three times quickly)

Betty Botter bought some butter but she said this butter's bitter,

If I put it in my batter it will make my batter bitter,

So 'twas better Betty Botter bought a bit of better butter to put in her batter.

———————

Peter Piper picked a peck of pickled pepper.

Did Peter Piper pick a peck of pickled pepper?

If Peter Piper picked a peck of pickled pepper,

Where's the peck of pickled pepper Peter Piper picked?

———————

She sells sea shells on the sea shore.

The shells she sells are sea shells I'm sure.

If she sells sea shells on the sea shore, where are the seashore shells she sells?

———————

Swan swam over the sea.

Swim, swan, swim.

Swan swam back again,

Well swum swan!

Moses supposes his toeses are roses, but Moses supposes erroneously.

For nobody's toeses are posies of roses as Moses supposes his toeses to be.[8]

The Three R's of Voice Projection

While tongue twisters can improve the clarity of your speech, the power and quality of the physical vibration (resonance) of your voice requires a different type of practice. Producing a strong and full-bodied sound (projecting your voice) is an important skill which affects both your credibility and audibility. To your listeners, your voice projection reflects your sincerity, your character, and your conviction. It also impacts on how you feel, as well as how you help your listeners to feel. Your projection reflects your attitude toward your audience and the ideas you are presenting. It will affect how people respond to your message and will increase your ability to be heard in meetings, in large rooms, or in noisy environments. A strongly-projected voice gives you the ability to fill the room and command the space.

To cultivate your voice projection, focus on "the three r's": release, respiration, and resonance. Doing these simple exercises for even just a few minutes a day before your important presentations and conversations can dramatically improve your speaking voice confidence and effectiveness over time.

1. Release

When your body is relaxed yet alert, you generate the optimum level of tension to create an energised voice. To achieve this state, we want to release tension as opposed to relaxing. Relaxation implies a total letting go, more like a collapse. Instead, you want to be free of unnecessary tension while holding a sufficient level of tension to keep yourself poised while standing or sitting upright, alert and focussed. You can release excess tension in your voice and body by:

- **Yawning**

- **Sighing**

- **Shaking** (try mimicking a shiver with your body and lips ("Brrrr") or imagine you are an Olympic swimmer getting ready to dive off the starting block – shake loose your arms and hands, legs and feet)

- **Massaging your TMJ joint** (your temporomandibular joint is a hinge that connects your jaw to the temporal bones of your skull, which are in front of each ear)

- **Sticking out and stretching your tongue** in a hissing snake-like move

- **Swinging your arms** freely back and forth as you bend your knees with each downswing. Straighten your knees on each upswing in a light bouncing motion.

2. Respiration

When you breathe fully and deeply, you begin to lower your stress hormones such as adrenaline and cortisol. As you calm and centre yourself through slower, more consciously deeper breathing, your voice also becomes fuller and more authoritative.

Here is a way you can practise breathing more fully and naturally:

- Place one hand on your chest and one hand over your lower abdomen

- Exhale all your air as if you are blowing out a candle

- At the end of a full exhale, drop your jaw and relax your belly

- Allow the air to stream in with your natural inhaling reflex

You should feel your belly move and expand with air with each in breath before your chest rises. This will indicate that you are allowing a full, deep breath.

3. Resonance

Resonance is the physical reverberation of your voice. It is what gives your voice a full-bodied sound of authority and warmth. Resonance helps you deliver your message with power and impact. There are two kinds of vocal resonance relevant for effective speaking: chest resonance and mask resonance.

The resonance in your chest area is used more often for one-on-one conversations, whereas the resonance in your 'mask' or nose/cheekbone area is more applicable for presentations and projecting to a larger audience. A chest resonance creates a more intimate, conversational tone. To feel your chest resonance, practise speaking as if your mouth is located on your chest so the sound is being projected out through your sternum. Start with a long 'Ahhhhhhhhh' sound on the exhale and feel your sternum vibrate as you begin speaking.

Mask resonance is useful when you want to project to groups or larger audiences. Mask resonance creates a more strongly projected tone and carries your voice further and more powerfully. To feel your mask resonance, practise speaking as if your voice is projecting from an imaginary mask area around your eyes and cheekbones. This may sound unusual, but give this a try: to locate your mask resonance, try making a long 'meoooowww' sound as if you are a cat. In order to avoid sounding overly nasal, you can lift your soft palate as if you are smelling a rose or hiding a small plum inside your mouth as you are about to speak.

Practise feeling the two resonances (chest and mask) and notice the different sensations. When you are preparing to speak in public, practise your mask resonance exercises to warm yourself up to make a powerful impact.

The Five Vocal Dynamics of Expressive Speaking (Prosody)

We have all had the experience of listening to a monotonous speaker. It is easy to drift off and disengage from their message when their sound is droning on and on. By contrast, a powerful speaker will engage the audience by practising what I call the five vocal dynamics or what is technically known as prosody (vocal dynamics). Prosody refers to the movements of your voice from one quality to another. You can remember the five vocal dynamics using this mnemonic phrase – Very Pretty, Pretty, Pretty Lady.

The five vocal dynamics are:

Volume, Pace, Pitch, Pause and Length.

Your volume can vary from a soft to a louder sound.

Your pace can range from a slow to a faster speed of speaking.

Your pitch is can fluctuate from low to high tones.

Your pauses create silent space between your words to highlight your message.

The length stretches from short to long (clipped to elongated words).

Some effective ways to develop your prosody are reading children's stories, reciting poetry, or through marking up your draft presentation script with notes of where you want to change your vocal dynamics. By developing your awareness and skill with the five basic dynamics of your voice, you can powerfully increase your expressiveness and consequently your ability to engage your audience.

Also, beware of what is called 'upspeak' in varying your pitch. Upspeak is the tendency to end your sentences in an upward lilt as if you are asking a question instead of making a statement. This habit may be formed in an attempt to avoid criticism. Although you may think you are taking less of a risk by ending in a higher-pitched questioning intonation, you risk undermining your authority. In New Zealand, however, upspeak is a common habit, so it does not always indicate a lack of confidence. It could instead be a sign of your collaborative intention or a cultural norm.

A Stanford University study by psychologists Guillory and Gruenfeld looked at the impact of the pace of speaking on how participants feel. They hypothesised that taking up more time with our voices is a way of claiming social space. If we do not rush our words and we are not afraid to pause, it is as if we feel deserving of the time we are using. Slower speech demonstrates a sort of openness. When you speak more slowly, you run the risk of being interrupted, so slower speech may indicate a lack of fear of interruptions. Participants in their study reported that they felt more powerful, confident, and effective when they were reading a speech slowly (on a banner moving across a computer screen) than when they were reading a more quickly moving banner.[9]

Practice Readings

Pick a favourite poem or an inspirational speech to practise your vocal expressiveness. Two of my favourites include, *The Journey*[10] by Mary Oliver and, *Where Many Rivers Meet*[11] by David Whyte. *The Journey* relates directly to speaking your truth in a powerful way and claiming your voice. The poem *Where Many Rivers Meet* expresses eloquently the interconnectedness of all life. I recommend memorising one or two of your favourite poems. Through memorisation you are freed from reading and can more fully practise expressing yourself in a powerful way. Alternatively, choose a newspaper or magazine and experiment with reading the letters to the editor out loud. These letters are generally passionate opinions and so lend themselves to expressive speaking.

Voicing Your Boundaries

Sue was an aspiring leader in her organisation in a role that was supposed to involve organisational strategy. She realised, however, that she was being perceived more like an executive assistant who could pick up the little jobs that no-one else wanted to handle. Sue realised she would need to start voicing some firmer boundaries in terms of the tasks she would accept. She decided to intentionally stop agreeing to work that was outside of her designated role. She began standing up for herself as opposed to always jumping in to support others' projects.

Rebecca, however, had the opposite issue. She resisted taking on any work outside of her job description. The rest of her team started feeling resentful because she was not demonstrating concern for the group. Rebecca was letting the rest of them deal with unexpected issues which arose and not pitching in herself. People will respect your integrity when you clearly voice your boundaries, however if you never stretch and make the occasional exception, you could be perceived by others as being overly individualistic rather than a team player. Reflect on your boundaries. How firm or flexible are they? Which boundaries would you like to strengthen and which boundaries would you like to stretch?

Actively Engage Your Voice

The life energy you activate through engaging your voice will greatly support your development of the other five keys to presence, influence, and creative confidence. I recommend you continue to work with the voice exercises as you move on to explore the next keys and activities.

Your voice will also grow stronger when supported by a clear vision. Building your vision is the next foundation we will address in developing your voice of leadership.

"My voice is beating

on the drum in your ear. . .

don't think that's a casual thing."

Unknown

Key # 1 Summary:

- ✓ Research confirms widespread vocal suppression

- ✓ Shame, arrogance, and a fear of ostracism may block your voice

- ✓ Confident speakers are passionate, insightful, and collaborative

- ✓ Vocal articulation, projection, and prosody enhance your authority

- ✓ Speak up to delineate your boundaries or step up to stretch them

Vision

Vision without action is a daydream ... Action without vision is a nightmare
Japanese proverb

A couple of years ago, I learned a painful lesson which made me realise the importance of maintaining my vision no matter what I am doing. I was preparing to facilitate a leadership course for over 200 managers at one of New Zealand's largest organisations. The theme of the course was centred on developing the leadership team's ability to grasp the wider implications of their organisation's current situation and the bigger picture. A few days before the event, I began preparing myself. I spent eight full hours painstakingly matching the PowerPoint slide numbers to the workbook page numbers. I was focussed on getting the details right and making sure I knew exactly which slide went with which page. I spent an entire day with my nose buried in minutiae. I was determined to be thoroughly prepared.

Shortly before the event, I received an updated workbook and PowerPoint slides from the course development team. To my dismay, I noticed that the page numbers had been shifted. The relevant workbook page numbers I had carefully input on the approximately 50 original PowerPoint slides were now mismatched with the workbook. All my detailed work ended up having been a waste of my time. I was extremely frustrated at the time, but later I had a good laugh at the irony of me leading a workshop all about focusing on the 'big picture' vision, while I was more concerned with the tiny details. I spent the rest of my limited preparation time choosing to put my attention instead on the larger concepts I would be explaining. I reminded myself of why I was facilitating the course in the first place; namely for the organisation's leaders to clarify their vision.

Keeping Your Vision in Sight

How well do you manage to keep your attention on the bigger picture or on the larger context of any given situation? Do you often lose sight of your vision or get distracted by seemingly endless details? As a leader, you are a guiding light and wayshower for others. Ideally, you inspire and empower people with your vision, transforming their lack of clarity and confidence into hopefulness and resolve in moving forward. Whether your work involves leading a team or leading yourself, do you ever stop to think about how many balls you need to juggle at once? It is not easy to stay focussed on your vision and mission while you are trying to manage so many details as well. Take a moment to think about all the areas of your business or career that you need to keep your eye on. Chances are you probably have ten or more priorities to handle as a leader, an entrepreneur, salesperson, or jobseeker.

Here are some of the balls you may be juggling: marketing, sales, finances, administration, professional development, competition, technology, research, the economy, compliance, taxes, and so on. How are you managing to juggle all of these areas? If you are like most of us, you drop a few balls from time to time. It is impossible to keep your eye on all the important things at once.

If you find yourself overwhelmed with all you have to handle, I recommend refocussing on the primary reason you are doing what you are doing. When you are focussed on the larger context, the details will likely seem less crushing. Yes, the details are important, but they should not cause you to lose sight of the bigger picture.

You are the Guardian of Your Vision

As a leader, you are the steward of your life's direction as well as your organisation's direction. You are the one keeping yourself and your team moving together in a unified way. You are the guardian of the greater vista, a source of insight, inspiration, and motivation to others who may lose the big picture from time to time.

As you are managing so many different areas in life and work, it is powerful to spend some time clarifying your own foundational vision which underpins everything you do. In 2011, Geoff Macdonald, the Ideas Architect from Australia, helped me to clarify my leadership vision. Geoff challenged me to answer the following two questions: 1). What is the only problem in the world, and, 2). What is my solution? I pondered these questions and came up with answers which I hope inspire you to reflect on your own view of the only problem in the world and your unique way of solving it. I decided that the only problem in the world, the one that underlies all other problems, is a false sense of separation. This is the same problem you find in your family, your community, your organisation, and your world. This sense of disconnection is an illusion. Science has proven that all energy in the universe is interconnected. The essence of every single atom is the same – pure energy. We are all at the core that same energy in different forms. My solution to solve this sense of separation is to help people connect with themselves and others. I support people in three areas which impact their lives both at home and at work: powerful presentation, courageous conversation, and creative collaboration. In short, I help people to connect with and express their voice of leadership.

After Geoff asked me to decide on the only problem in the world from my perspective, he asked me to come up with the '10 commandments' of my philosophy; what he called my manifesto. I list my 10 commandments here as I firmly believe they will help you to fully express your own voice of leadership.

1. **Be here now** – Being present, fully awake and focussed on what is occurring in the moment enables you to respond most resourcefully.

2. **Breathe** – By consciously. breathing deeply and fully, you enhance your self-awareness and your ability to relax and be your most resourceful self.

3. **Listen to your intuition** – By listening to your inner voice, you build self-trust and more easily make the right choices and respond appropriately in each situation.

4. **Seek to empathise and understand** – Everyone wants to be more deeply understood. If you listen with compassion and seek to understand what is going on for others, you will strengthen your relationships and sense of connection.

5. **Be open to change** – Life is constantly changing. By developing an open-minded, open-hearted attitude, you can flex and flow with life and often find solutions that are better than your original plans.

6. **Build Trust** – Take care to meet needs, manage expectations and keep promises.[1] These three foundations are critical to building trust in yourself, your relationships, and in your organisations.

7. **Speak the truth** – Speak up authentically and directly, with kindness as well as honesty and discernment.

8. **Collaborate** – We live in an interconnected world. Our efforts together are so much more powerful than our efforts alone. Seek out ways to work together with others to create a better outcome for all.

9. **Appreciate and celebrate often** – Take time to share your love and praise with others as well as to honour achievements, discoveries, and mistakes. Take time to mourn losses suffered and to rejoice in larger dreams realised.

10. **Honour the cycles and the seasons** – There is a time to sow and a time to reap. There is the time of new life in the spring, the time of fullness in the summer, and the time of darkness, death and stillness in the winter. These seasons happen in our relationships and projects as well. Honour the ebb and flow of life. Realise it is okay to adjust your pace of living to align with what is happening at the time.

Your personal voice of leadership vision is a picture you hold of your best possible self in the world. In order to have a positive impact on others, what kind of energy and attitude will you need to hold? How will you need to act?

Have these 10 commandments sparked any insights for you? Reflect on your own experience in life. I challenge you to honour your unique perspective by articulating your own philosophy.

What Is Your Philosophy?

As an exercise to develop your own philosophy, consider the following:

1. What is your opinion of the biggest problem in the world?

2. How do you help solve it?

3. What would be your 10 commandments if someone put you in charge of the world?

Strategic Illustration

Strategic illustration[2] is a process that works by giving you a visual picture of where you are currently to where you ideally would like to be. Words are processed by our short-term memory, whereas images go directly into our long-term memory where they stick more permanently. One study found that after three days, only 10-20 percent of written or spoken information was retained compared with a retention rate of almost 65 percent for visual information.[3] Also, your brain emits serotonin and oxytocin when you draw and dream. Your brain has trouble telling the difference between what is real and what is imagined, so it produces 'feel-good' neurotransmitters when you are visualising your ideal scenario through drawing it. You do not have to be a 'good' artist. Even stick figures and simple symbols will do the trick. I have found for myself as well as for my clients, that drawing symbols instead of words can boost memory and creativity. It is also more enjoyable to draw a visual map instead of memorising every word.

Engage Your Whole Brain

To activate the full power of your vision, you want to intentionally activate your whole brain. The left side of your brain is associated with a sequential and analytic processing style. It recognises serial events like talking, writing and reading. The right side of the brain is integrative. It finds connections and interprets images and emotions. The two sides of the brain work together to process information. By combining words with images, you fire up both sides of the brain simultaneously to create a more tangible, compelling vision. The synthesising process of the left and right sides of the brain is critical to accessing the deep clarity needed to create change. A powerful example of integrating the often-neglected right side of the brain is expressed in Jill Bolte Taylor's 2008 TED talk, entitled My Stroke of Insight.[4] Taylor had a stroke during which the left side of her brain, the logical, analytical side, was temporarily paralysed. She describes the incredible sense of awe, wonder, and connection she felt when only her creative, emotional, right side of the brain was working.

Your Voice of Leadership Vision

Here is an exercise to engage the creative right side of your brain as well as the verbal left side of your brain. On a piece of paper or in a journal notebook, draw a sketch to represent your personality as you think you are currently perceived by others (stick figures or symbols are fine). Then, next to that picture or on another page, draw a picture of how you would like to be perceived when you have developed your new voice of leadership.

Your Voice of Leadership Declaration

After creating a visual representation of your current and ideal self-image, create a voice of leadership declaration to go along with the image of how you would like to be perceived by others. This voice of leadership declaration is a self-affirmation or a personal brand statement which will support you stepping into the self-image you that you know deep down is authentically you. Here are a few examples of voice of leadership declarations:

"I am a clear, confident, cultural change agent, connecting with a strong voice of leadership."

"I am a confident, collaborator making powerful connections."

"I am a friendly, playful, and intelligent connector with a strong voice."

Once you create your declaration, I suggest you repeat it to yourself often as you go about your daily routine. It is especially powerful to say this to yourself just before you go into an important meeting or give a presentation. By persistently and consistently repeating your declaration to yourself, you will begin to automatically display behaviours consistent with your desired self-image. Affirming your declaration silently to yourself upon waking or upon going to sleep are two other potent times when your subconscious is most receptive to the self-image you are aiming to embed in your consciousness. I suggest you write your declaration at the bottom of your voice of leadership ideal drawing and place it somewhere where you will see it often.

Rewiring Your Brain

Be patient. It takes a lot of repetition to 'rewire' your brain. You can literally strengthen the neural pathways in your brain which will activate your presence and creative confidence as you enter into challenging communication situations. Once you clarify your voice of leadership vision and declaration, you are on your way to becoming a positive and influential leader. I have had many clients report, and experienced myself, that the voice of leadership declaration will come to mind and provide inspiration and support in challenging situations when it is most needed.

Crafting Your Purpose Statement

Another vision-strengthening step is to craft your purpose statement. This statement is a strong message which gives specific direction to your particular strengths, talents, actions, and desired outcomes.

Here is a short, simple process to help you clarify your purpose. It will help you to identify and value your unique contribution to the world. In as little as ten minutes, you can create your own focussed purpose statement to boost your inspiration and motivation. Any time you need to refocus or to re-energise yourself, you can revisit this exercise.

1. Identify Your Best Qualities

To begin, take a minute to brainstorm all of your best qualities and make a list. Now, pick just three of those qualities which you believe are your three top qualities. List those three qualities and condense each quality into one word. For example, your quality words could be words like positivity, empathy, enthusiasm, and generosity. For example, if you are a person who is curious and engaged in conversation with others, you could condense that trait into the word 'interest'. Your quality words could include traits like determination, empathy, enthusiasm, generosity, humour, or positivity.

2. Identify Your Favourite Activities

After you have chosen your three quality words, write down three ways you enjoy expressing those qualities with others, using one action word for each of the three ways. For example, if one of your quality words is humour, you may enjoy expressing that through socialising with others. You could condense that activity down to one word such as 'connecting'. Other action words or verbs you might use for ways of expressing could be words like coaching, networking, planning, researching, writing, speaking, and so on.

3. Fill in Your Purpose Statement Template

To complete your purpose statement, plug in your six words (three qualities and three activities) into the following template:

Your Purpose Statement Template

My purpose is to express my _____ (quality 1), _____ (quality 2), and _____ (quality 3) through _____ (activity 1), _____ (activity 2), and_____ (activity 3) (with) others.

Purpose Statement Example

My purpose is to express my <u>positivity</u>, <u>humour</u>, and <u>drive</u> through <u>planning</u>, <u>networking</u>, and <u>collaborating</u> with others.

You can create a strong and focussed affirmation through crafting your purpose statement, which will help you to fully step into your voice of leadership vision and declaration.

Once you have created your purpose statement, it can be helpful to shorten it into a catchy phrase similar to a movie title. Make it short and sweet and easy to remember. I picked up this clever tip back in 2010 from a former coaching colleague, Steve Wooderson, and I still recommend it today.

Here are some of the phrases that my clients have created to help them remember their purpose:

- 'Making Powerful Connections'

- 'Sarah Sparking Insights'

- 'Igniting Possibilities'

- 'Clear, Confident, Collaborator'

- 'Playful, Powerful Presence'

- 'Laser Light Clarity'

Your purpose statement is a work in progress which can shift and change with your evolving direction. Do not worry about getting it right. I recommend you write out your purpose statement and post your movie titles where they will be easily visible and you can read them often. They will give you energy and vision to live your passionate purpose each day, inspiring others as you do. Remember, too, even though you are on an important mission, you can also have fun with the process. In fact, enjoying your work is a good indicator that you are on the right path.

Backwards Visioning Process

Another way to strengthen your vision of how you would like to express your voice of leadership is through a process called 'Backwards Visioning'. This process begins with you creating an ideal image of your best possible self in twenty years' time. Imagine that everything has gone as well as it possibly could. You have worked hard and succeeded at accomplishing all of your life goals. The next step is to write about what you visualised. Then imagine where you will be along the path towards your grand vision in ten years' time and make some notes. Working backwards, you clarify your vision in stages, writing next about your vision in five years from now, then two years from now, then next year, in six months from now, three months from now, next month, next week, tomorrow and today. By working in reverse order from the future to the present, you create a larger context and meaning for your daily and weekly activities. Whether or not this particular future transpires is not important. The fact that you are actively engaging your positive expectancy and imagination is what energises and motivates you in your daily life. I suggest you do not view this process as a goal-setting activity. Rather, this is an exercise to expand your vision and to infuse meaning into your daily activities.

Timeframe	Date	Age	Voice of Leadership Vision
In 20 years from today	2037	76	Enjoying writing, mentoring, teaching, and speaking in a spacious and balanced way – feeling grateful for a full sense of contribution and community, belonging here in Tamaki Makaurau (Auckland) as well as with my wider international whanau/ family/ network.
In 10 Years	2027	66	Happy to be living with a satisfying balance between our city and country homes. Loving having online international and local connections as well as continuing my writing, mentoring and speaking. Now, my online courses are popular as well as my live engagements.
In 5 Years	2022	61	My book is now opening doors for me to engage with a wider audience – happy to be able to get back to my hometown more often for family visits. Loving making a contribution and feeling connected here in Tāmaki Makaurau, Auckland, across Oceania and internationally.
In 2 Years	2019	58	I am thrilled that I have successfully consolidated my voice of leadership tools and stories into the physical form of a book. I have sold thousands of copies and booked speaking engagements, workshops and group/ individual mentoring clients with various organisations and individuals, locally and abroad. Social media has been extremely effective at spreading the word and advertising my book and my work.
By Next Year	Jun. 2018	57	I love all the connections I have made in my book writing and publishing endeavours. I have formed new collaborations with local and international colleagues and organisations and have booked speaking engagements online as well as in the States. Enjoying travel with my partner to visit our families overseas while combining our visit with professional work.

Timeframe	Date	Age	Voice of Leadership Vision
In 6 Months	Oct 2017	56	I have a beautiful, quality published book that people are happily buying here in Aotearoa, New Zealand as well as internationally. I have a whole team of people who are collaborating with me in spreading the word and distributing my mentoring programs and books. My book is proving to be a powerful asset in terms of booking speaking engagements and attracting new clients.
In 3 Months	Jul. 2017	56	My finished book is in my hands! It has been edited, proofed, designed, typeset and has a fantastic cover design. I am delighted to spread the word about it on social media and to my contacts/clients. I am excited to now have a powerful tool to share with clients old and new.
Next Month	Jun. 2017	56	I am feeling good about how everything is flowing so smoothly in putting this book together. I am pleased to have had an excellent editor and proofreader, designer, and printer all working to help this book be excellent. I have a distributor lined up, and I have sold many pre-order copies already to existing clients.
Next Week	May 2017	56	I am working with the proofreader to finish the last polishing aspects of the book and I am meeting with the printer and designer to begin the next stages of publishing.
Tomorrow	7 May 2017	56	I am finishing incorporating my edits on Chapters 5 and 6 into my manuscript and feeling well-prepared to send it to my proofreader next week. I am happily preparing for my group mentoring event next week as well.
Today	6 May 2017	56	Continue to finish my editing on Chapters 2 and 3 and then take a break for a nice relaxing and healthy dinner with my partner.

When you are living every day with a greater sense of meaning, your presence, influence, and creativity are destined to grow and evolve. As life has a way of bringing us unexpected twists and turns in the road, you could choose to create several scenarios based on different long-term visions you could imagine. Here is one example of a backwards visioning process:

Through this backward visioning process, you can maintain your motivation to handle some of the less glamourous details of your life and work as you keep your eye on the bigger picture.

Use Pictures to Magnify Your 'Voice of Leadership' Vision

When I was 35 and living in Boulder, Colorado, I wanted to test out the power of using pictures to manifest my dreams. My son was only three years old and we did not have much spare cash at the time. Still, I had an urge to visit England and Scotland as I was discovering that my ancestors were from that part of the world and I wanted to feel a closer connection. I visited our local travel agency and picked up some travel brochures from the area, cutting out pictures of castles, rolling hills, and various ancient sites that attracted me. I pasted the photos onto a piece of cardboard and hung them up by my desk where I could see them every day. I enjoyed looking at them but did not know how in the world I would get to England, given our current financial situation.

Soon after I did this, my husband announced to me that there was a storytelling course in England that he wanted to attend. I figured he would save up and go there in a few years. I had no immediate plans to travel and no budget. To my surprise, my husband encouraged me to take a big leap and we were flying to England the very next month, in time for the start of the storytelling course. I thought we were crazy, yet my intuition was egging me on, telling me to go through with the trip anyway. Within a matter of months from when I first tacked up the English photos on the wall, I was living in an old castle-like estate looking out over rolling hills! We ended up putting our house in Boulder on the market and selling it to finance our trip. The plan was that we would live in England for a few years while my husband got his storytelling and teaching degree and I would continue to study and teach voice. Although we ended up coming back to Boulder sooner than we thought and moving to Maui (another story), I certainly learned about the power of visualisation to activate reality, often more quickly than logic would suggest.

A previous coaching client of mine who is now a successful entrepreneur swears by the process of visualisation. She even runs workshops teaching others the value of visualisation, having found the process to be extremely effective in her own life and work.

Free Flowing Writing

If you are feeling stuck on a problem, feeling a lack of inspiration and vision, or wanting to accelerate your creative insights, stream of consciousness writing can be particularly helpful. The free-flowing writing technique involves writing non-stop in longhand form for a set timeframe or for a certain number of pages. I like to set my watch for 15 minutes and to follow this process whenever I want to get my creative juices flowing. Through unedited, free-flowing stream of consciousness writing, you become familiar with all the unspoken chatter of your mind and can clearly see what is bothering you, what your dominant thoughts are, what you feel, and so on. The idea is that you do not stop writing until you have reached your goal of a certain number of pages or a certain time limit. If you feel stuck and puzzled about what to write, just keep going, even writing, "don't know what to say, feeling stuck, stuck, stuck, yuck, I don't like doing this . . . " and then, something else will come to mind. Just write until you feel that you have cleared yourself of enough superficial mind chatter to unveil your deeper thoughts, feelings and important priorities. You will be surprised at the spring of creativity which comes surging up from what you thought was a dry well.

Envision Your Best Possible Self

This well-researched exercise has been shown to boost positive emotions, optimism, hope, coping skills and to strengthen positive expectations about the future. Set aside 15-20 minutes of uninterrupted time for yourself. Visualise yourself at a future moment in time, having realised your professional and life goals and having the ideal character strengths which you have honed over the years. You could choose to imagine a time six months, one year, five years, or even 10 years from now. You decide what time period you are most drawn to visualise. Then, imagine your best possible self and how you are feeling now that you have reached this point in time. Imagine it in detail where you have worked hard and succeeded at reaching an important milestone or realising one of your long-cherished dreams. The point is not to drift off into fantasy, but rather, to think of things which are positive and attainable within reasonable possibility. After you have managed to create a fairly clear image in your mind, write about the details. Writing the ideal scenario of your best possible self creates a logical structure for the future and can help you move from the realm of fuzzy ideas to real possibilities. After you have created a positive image of your future self, commit to writing continuously for 15-20 minutes about what you imagine your future to be.

Make sure to write about how you are feeling and your character strengths, not just what you are doing in your imagined future. What personal qualities will you need to activate and develop to make this best possible self a reality? Do not worry about getting the grammar and spelling right. The point is to strengthen your image of the positive, powerful self you have successfully created. Because life is an adventure, and not a predictable path, it is important to hold this exercise lightly, as an inspiration rather than a fixed plan. Remember what Joseph Campbell, the famous mythologist said, "If you can see your path laid out in front of you step by step, you know it is not your path. Your own path you make with every step you take". Your vision will unfold and evolve as you follow your inspiration day by day.

Decode Your Dreams for Inspiration

One of the most powerful ways to get in touch with your creative inspiration and visionary nature is to start paying attention to what is revealed in your nightly dreams. The scientific study of dreams is called oneirology. (This term is derived from the Greek word *oneiron* which means dream). Although oneirology is focussed on the quantitative study of dreams, many ancient societies, such as those in Egypt and Greece, considered dreaming a supernatural communication or a means of divine intervention. Thousands of years ago, ancient Egyptians used the messages in their dreams in order to cure illnesses, make important State decisions and even to decide where to build a temple or when to wage a battle.[5] The famous story of Jeanne d'Arc (Joan of Arc) also demonstrates the respectful status that dreams were given in our history. Joan was so connected to her 'voices,' or what we may today call her intuition or guidance, that she persuaded the Dauphin (heir to the throne of France) Charles VI, to allow her to lead the French army against the English at Orléans when she was only 18.[6] Today with our society's rational, scientific bias, many people tend not to value the symbolism or inspiration found in dreams. However, we can benefit by making room for both reason and intuition to inspire our 'voice of leadership.'

In their book *Wayfinding Leadership: Groundbreaking Wisdom for Developing Leaders*, authors Chellie Spiller, Hoturoa Barclay-Kerr, and John Panoho refer to a holistic approach which encompasses both the rational and the intuitive as 'sphere intelligence' as opposed to 'square intelligence' which honours only rational thinking.

If you engage in an open exploration with the images which present themselves to you in your dreams, you will access powerful material to fuel your creativity. The following activity is recommended for a deeper dive into your intuitive wisdom and a closer look at your subconscious programmes. In time, with patience and persistence, your dreams can become a rich source of creative inspiration and insight.

Tips to Remember Your Dreams

Even if you just remember one image or one snippet of a dream, you can still glean some important revelations. I suggest keeping a notebook by your bed with a small flashlight and pen, so that you can easily jot down your dream upon waking. If you can avoid using a buzzing alarm which could jar you from your dream, that would be ideal. Preferably, use some soft music to wake up to instead. I have found dream-work to be a powerful tool for both myself and my mentoring clients when we want to get more insight into a particularly challenging issue or change. Dreams can provide subtle and sometimes dramatic 'aha' moments which may not be as easily accessible with normal waking consciousness.

"It is a common experience
that a problem difficult at night
is resolved in the morning after the committee
of sleep has worked on it."

John Steinbeck, Sweet Thursday

Your Dream-work Process

It is quite normal to go through long periods of not remembering any of your dreams. However, when you are working through a difficult transition or want clarity on your direction or your feelings about a situation, your dreams can be a source of powerful guidance.

Here is the process I recommend to help you work with your dreams. I suggest you give yourself at least a week to get the hang of it. It can often take a few days to begin remembering your dreams if you have not been in the habit of cultivating them.

Step One: Before you go to bed, set the intention to receive information or guidance in your dream regarding a current challenge or situation.

Step Two: Upon waking, give your dream a title, a first phrase that comes to mind, as if it were the title of a movie.

Step Three: Jot down any feelings you remember from the dream.

Step Four: Write your dreams in the present tense...I am seeing, I am running, and so on.

Step Five: Replace the names of people, places and objects in the dream with an x. For example – I am running towards x and reaching x.

Step Six: Describe each x (person, place, or thing) in your dream as if you were describing it to someone from another planet. For example, a house is a structure or protective shelter that I live in.

Step Seven: Write out what you like and do not like about each x. For example, what I like about a house – it is safe, secure, and protective. What I dislike about a house – it is confining, and takes a lot of maintenance.

Step Eight: Ask yourself: "Is there anything literally speaking to me in my dream that requires an action in the physical world?" Dreams are often symbolic and sometimes, they are literal. Only you can discern the dream's messages for yourself.

Step Nine: If you want to hear a different perspective, you could share your dream with a trusted friend or colleague. Ask them to tell you what the dream would mean to them if it were theirs. Sometimes getting another perspective can shed light on a different angle than you originally considered yourself.

Step Ten: After completing the above process, what impressions do you have about the message in your dream? You are the ultimate authority on your own intuition. What actions, if any, is the dream telling you to take?

Dream Recall can be Cyclical

Many people say they do not remember their dreams. However, through setting an intention to receive guidance from your dreams, your recall will become stronger in time. It is natural to go through periods of not remembering, however, with practice and openness to receive your dreams they will become more accessible to you. The more attention you pay to your dreams, the more value you will gain from their messages. One helpful practise I have found is to keep a file of important dream titles and to review them from time to time. Through reviewing your dream titles, you will get a sense of underlying themes in your life and gain possible clues to best next steps to help you align more closely with your purpose.

Key # 2 Summary:

- ✓ Keep your eyes on the bigger picture
- ✓ Your voice of leadership vision, purpose, and slogans will keep you on track
- ✓ Use strategic illustration to engage whole brain creativity
- ✓ Backwards visioning gives flexible direction to your present activities
- ✓ Decode your dreams for deeper insight

3

Values

Anthony Casalena started the content management system company, Squarespace, by himself in his university dorm room. It is now a successful startup regularly voted as one of the best places to work in New York City.[1] Its company culture is one that is flat, open and creative. A flat organisation is one where there are no (or very few) levels of management in between staff and executives. SquareSpace also offers robust benefits and perks, including 100 percent coverage of health insurance, flexible vacations, attractive office space, catered meals, stocked kitchens, monthly celebrations, relaxation spaces and periodic guest lecturers. Down-to-earth leaders and direct access to management have a great deal of impact on the culture as well.

The flat structure and benefits provided by Squarespace reflect the organisation's values of autonomy, respect, and empowerment for employees.[2] Clear values which support the well-being of people directly impact on success as the research indicates. In their book, 'Firms of Endearment,' Raj Sisodia and co-authors showed that organisations who are led by clear values and a strong sense of purpose outperformed the S&P 500 in cumulative returns by 14 times over a period of 15 years from 1998-2013. (The S&P 500 is widely regarded as the most accurate gauge of the performance of large U.S.-based organisations).

Studies suggest that with clear, committed values you will be more successful in your endeavours. Through examining, clarifying and expressing your values, you will have a stronger voice of leadership. Clear values can help you direct your energy more intentionally, make better decisions and take more aligned actions. Through your words and actions, you create, embed, evolve, and sustain your values and have an impact on others in your organisation. [3]

Clear Values Inspire Courage to Change

Getting in touch with your deeply held values can radically change your life. Some of my mentoring clients ended up leaving their jobs after going through a process of values clarification.

They realised that their roles and organisations did not support them living in alignment with their core values of integrity and respect.

Maia was in a middle management role. She realised through our mentoring process that the value of integrity was what she rated most highly. She was struggling to feel comfortable being herself at work and expressing her authentic voice. Her manager and senior leaders had different expectations of what constituted a proper work ethic and Maia was always feeling an underlying tension. Through engaging in some values clarification exercises, Maia realised that she was part of a new generation of leaders who like to prioritise work-life balance. She would need to set some boundaries in terms of how many hours she was willing to spend at work. Her boss had the habit of a workaholic and expected others to work as he did. He had the habit of putting in long hours and working hard while giving lip service to the ideal of work-life balance. When Maia identified her core values of integrity, health, and harmony, she ended up making a courageous choice to leave that organisation. After moving through her fear of change, she experienced a new level of energy and inner strength which came from committing to living in alignment with her core values.

Resolving Conflicting Values

Anika was another client who learned the painful cost of living out of alignment with her values. She accepted a job thinking it would provide her with a sense of security. However, it did not strongly support her sense of direction. She thought if she took the position for a year or two that it would lead her to more opportunities. In Anika's case, the price of prioritising her value of security over her values of creativity and social connection was a sense of stagnation and boredom. She felt stuck in this position. The job demanded that she work by herself on detailed accounting-like activities. She underestimated how incompatible this work would be with her outgoing, big picture personality. Anika eventually realised the price for supposed security was too high, and that actually, doing a job she did not enjoy was not secure anyway as her mental health was suffering. When she got in touch with the pain that this misalignment was causing, she summoned the courage to leave the job. She vowed never to put herself in that kind of position again, deciding that she would not settle for a job that did not support her living in harmony with her values or purpose. She left the organisation and found a job in sales and customer service which allowed her to express her values and strengths in social interaction.

Tom learned how to listen with discernment to uncomfortable feedback from a potential employer. He had been told by an interviewer that he was not 'tough' enough, perhaps 'too polite' for the role he was hoping to fill. By clarifying his core values of kindness and respect, he realised he did not want to change himself to adapt to that particular organisation's culture of crudeness which included a great deal of swearing.

An Historical Example of the Power of Values

One powerful, historical example of how clear values give strength and direction to one's life is the story of Archie and Millicent Baxter and their son, the New Zealand poet, James K. Baxter. In *The Memoirs of Millicent Baxter*, Millicent gives powerful testimony to the motivating and ennobling force of values. Her parents were of the intellectual elite; Professor John Macmillan Brown, one of the founding professors of Canterbury University College and Helen Connon, who served as principal of Christchurch Girls' School for 14 years and was the first woman to graduate with an MA with honours from the British Empire.

Archie, on the other hand was a poor farmer who had endured unimaginable torture by the New Zealand military on the front lines of France in World War I. As a conscientious objector he had refused to take part in the war and to kill against his will. Millicent had read a published letter that Archie had written to his parents, and his words transformed her whole outlook on politics and every other aspect of life. She felt compelled to meet him and sought him out where he was living with his five brothers and sisters on a farm in the south island of New Zealand. Archie was everything Millicent dreamed he would be in terms of how closely his life reflected his strong, peaceful values. Millicent's father, however, was not pleased with her attraction, as he judged Archie's background as a poor farmer to be unworthy of Millicent's elite upbringing. Millicent married Archie against her father's will, going to live with him in a primitive farm cottage with no electricity. People told her that the change in her way of living must have been like the fairytale of the princess and the peasant. "What they didn't know was that Archie was a prince," Millicent wrote. What had been done to him in the war had only strengthened his nobility of character. Millicent and Archie spent the rest of their lives together working for peace, passing on their peaceful values to their son, James K. Baxter, who became an award-winning poet. His poems reflect his deep passion for peace and social justice, which his parents undoubtedly passed onto him. In the case of the Baxters, the challenges they faced in opposition to their values ignited their determination to shine the light on those values even more brightly through how they lived their lives. The story of Archie and Millicent Baxter reminds me of the question posed by Spiller, Barclay-Kerr, and Panoho in their book *Wayfinding Leadership: Ground-breaking Wisdom for Developing Leaders*[4] – "As an ancestor of the future, what will be the wisdom you pass on?"

A Personal Lesson in Values

After leaving a corporate job in my 20s, I ventured into the world of professional acting. Encouraged by my early success in landing professional acting jobs I decided to pursue a Master of Fine Arts degree (MFA) in acting. I auditioned and was delighted to be offered a full scholarship to the professional acting programme at Pennsylvania State University. Not only would my tuition be covered for three years, I would actually be paid as well for teaching acting classes to undergraduate students. Before I accepted the offer, however, I received another acceptance letter from Rutgers University's Mason Gross School of the Arts, a school much closer to New York City, where I imagined I would be closer to 'success.' I would have to pay $24,000 for tuition and I would not be paid to teach acting. Also, my place in the programme was not guaranteed. I would have to prove myself each year in order to stay. So what did I do?

I ended up declining the full scholarship offer at Penn State where they warmly welcomed me, and instead I attended Rutgers where I had to pay and compete to be accepted. After just one term at Rutgers, I felt dejected and lost. I did not respond well to the acting teacher whose method was to yell at me to try to elicit emotion. In one particular class, I remember her yelling at me with the ultimate insult in front of my acting peers: "What's wrong with you! You're a rock. Don't you feeeel anything?" I certainly did feel – shame, embarrassment, and more fear. I froze!

Instead of being inspired, I felt beaten down. I withdrew from that programme feeling disillusioned and abandoned my dream of being a professional actor. I learned through that painful experience that I value a nurturing, supportive environment and that it is vital to be in a place where I feel encouraged rather than a place where I need to fight to prove I belong. I also learned that success is not defined by fame and fortune. It is defined by fulfillment, happiness, healthy social connections, and meaningful work.

At Rutgers, there was only one approach to acting, the Stanford Meisner Method. I learned that it is important to find the approach to life and work that fits you as an individual. Every teacher's approach is unique and what works for one may not work for another. I discovered through experiencing many alternative approaches to actor training, that there is no one method or path that is correct. It also clarified for me my values of health and well-being throughout this stressful period of my life. Consequently, I chose a new path where my health and well-being would be well-supported.

When I left acting school feeling dejected and with my proverbial tail between my legs, a friend of mine offered me a scholarship to a life-changing programme. As I was feeling lost and empty, I accepted her invitation and went along to a weekend seminar called 'Insight.' You have probably heard the saying, 'When one door closes, another one opens.' Fortunately, I found that to be the case. I was so inspired and moved by the training that I ended up attending all three levels of the Insight seminars which then led me to enrol in the University of Santa Monica's Spiritual Psychology programme. This programme challenged me to clarify my values and to commit to living in alignment with them. I was also asked to articulate my own theory of mental health. I identified 15 characteristics of psychological and emotional health and created a self-assessment tool which I still find valuable today. (See Appendix I)

Your Anger Highlights Your Values

Another effective way to clarify your values is to ask yourself what makes you angry. When your values are violated, your anger will be triggered. I notice that I feel angry whenever I perceive a lack of collaboration and inclusivity. For example, when I am at a meeting and certain people take up more than their fair share of airtime I can feel my irritation rising. Whenever I sense that one person is dominating, I feel angry. This action violates my value of reciprocity and fairness. What kind of situation triggers your anger? What values do those situations highlight for you? How does your experience of anger crystallise your values?

Get Honest with who You Are

Identifying and communicating your core values is a fundamental task of your voice of leadership.

Here are a few powerful activities to unveil your most passionate and precious values:

Take a look at what you are most focussed on in your life and work by answering the following 11 questions:

1. What inspires you most?

2. Which topics of conversation do you most engage in with others?

3. Where are you most disciplined in life and work?

4. What do you find yourself thinking about most of the time?

5. What do you imagine or visualise the most?

6. How does your living space reflect your values?

7. What do you spend your money on?

8. Where do you spend most of your energy?

9. What activity occupies most of your waking life?

10. What goals do you most often set for yourself?

11. What do you do which gives you the greatest satisfaction?

12. Considering your answers to the questions above, do you notice any patterns?

What core values emerge for you as you reflect? Are there inconsistencies between what you say you value and how you spend your life energy?

If so, you could choose to adjust your behaviour to align with your highest aspirations or you could get honest about what you actually value as reflected in your daily actions.

Take a moment to reflect on the quote below. How are your beliefs, thoughts, words, and actions reflected in your daily habits? Are they habits you want to keep?

> *"Your beliefs become your thoughts,*
> *Your thoughts become your words,*
> *Your words become your actions,*
> *Your actions become your habits,*
> *Your habits become your values,*
> *Your values become your destiny."*
>
> Mahatma Gandhi

Here is another exercise which will assist you in identifying your core values.

Values Challenge (Allow about 15 minutes or more to complete)

1. Read through the following steps before referring to the Table of Values on the next page.

2. Circle your ten most important values on the Table of Values.

3. Review your top ten circled values and select your top five values from that group. Place a * next to those values.

4. Consider your top five values and select your most important two values from that group.

5. Reflect on your top two values, then choose your number one value.

6. Consider how that value is currently present in your life and work. Does your personal brand reflect this top value? What changes could you make to align yourself with your number one value?

Table of Values

Acceptance	Change	Fun	Loyalty	Recognition
Accountability	Close relationships	Growth	Meaningful work	Religion
Achievement	Community	Harmony	Modesty	Reputation
Affection	Competition	Health	Nature	Security
Appreciation	Contribution	Honesty	Openness	Self-respect
Assertiveness	Cooperation	Humour	Order	Serenity
Authenticity	Creativity	Inclusivity	Peace	Silence
Authority	Democracy	Integrity	Personal development	Spirituality
Autonomy	Effectiveness	Intimacy	Play	Status
Awe	Empathy	Justice	Pleasure	Time
Beauty	Excellence	Knowledge	Power	Trust
Caring	Fame	Leadership	Privacy	Truth
Collaboration	Family	Location	Public Service	Wealth
Challenge	Freedom	Love	Purity	Wisdom

When you look at your top five values, what are you doing in your life which demonstrates those values? Are you actively living your values? Could a spy secretly following you detect your values by tracking your movements? Is there anything you want to stop doing, start doing, or continue to do with a more focussed intention?

Current Activity Log

This activity will give you a realistic picture of how you are spending your most valuable currency – your time. You can then evaluate if you want to change how you are spending that life energy.

Over the course of one week, keep a log of all your activities. Every time you switch to a new activity, first note the time and the number of minutes which you have just spent on the previous activity. At the end of the week you will have a clearer idea of just how you fill your precious days and how those activities reflect your values. You may be surprised at how you actually spend your time. Here is an example to get you started:

Current Activity Log

Date	Time	Activity	Duration	Values Reflected
Monday	7am	Swimming	1/2 Hour	Health
	8am	Cooking/ Eating Breakfast	1/2 Hour	Health
	9am	Checking Emails/ Correspondence	1 Hour	Connection
	10am	Writing Book	2 Hour	Contribution/ Mastery
	2pm	Mentoring Clients	2 Hour	Contribution/ Career/ Financial Well-Being
	5pm	Stretch/ Walk in Park	1/2 Hour	Health/ balance
	5.30pm	Dinner Prep	1/2 Hour	Health/ Family
	6pm	Dinner	1/2 Hour	Health/ Family

What did you discover about your most important activities and cherished values? Does the way you are living your life align with what you say are your values? If not, what will you do more of, less of, keep, start, or stop doing?

Embedding New Habits to Support Your Values

After completing the Values Challenge exercise, you may realise you need to embed more value-inspired habits into your life.

Here is an activity you can do to embed more value-inspired habits in your life. Write a list of up to five values you want to strengthen.

Ask yourself, "What can I do on a daily basis that will help me to actualise this value?" The size of the action is unimportant. What counts is the consistency of repetition until that activity comes automatically to you. There are various opinions of how many consecutive days it takes of repeating an action to form a habit. In 2009, a study by Phillipa Lally found that it takes 66 days for people to reach a level of self-reported automaticity with a habit.[5]

Key # 3 Summary:

✓ Clear values inspire courage to change

✓ Reflecting on and clarifying your values gives direction to your life and work

✓ Conflicting values cause stress and need to be addressed and resolved

✓ Values give you strength in standing up for what you believe

✓ Getting honest with your time helps you get honest about your values

✓ Your values are reflected in how you live your life

Vitality

You know those moments when you have a spring in your step? You feel alive and vibrant and totally at ease in yourself? When these moments become more the norm than the exception you are mastering the art of vitality. To build and sustain a strong voice, a clear vision and a life led by your highest values, you must nurture your vitality. Your vital energy is the fuel which will carry you forward and enhance your ability to make an impact in your chosen field. By supporting yourself physically, mentally, emotionally, and spiritually, you cultivate a radiant aliveness and exude a positive presence. Your vitality includes all aspects of your self-care, such as nurturing a positive attitude, self-awareness, self-acceptance, self-respect and self-compassion.

Self-Care

In order to embody your 'voice of leadership' vitality, your self-care must be impeccable. On all levels, including physically, mentally, emotionally, and spiritually, your self-care is the foundation of your energy and presence. Take an inventory of your current self-care practices and see which areas you want to improve. On the most basic physical level, how is your diet, your sleep and exercise habits? Mentally, do you challenge yourself with learning new skills and expanding your knowledge by reading? Emotionally, do you regularly connect with friends and engage in enjoyable recreational or creative activities? Spiritually, do you have practices like mindfulness, singing, dancing, prayer and/or inspirational reading that support you? Consider scheduling self-care activities in your diary to make sure you are giving them the time and attention they deserve.

Positivity

Positivity is another crucial contributor to your vitality. Positivity is an attitude of certainty, acceptance and affirmation. It is optimistic and constructive. Research by Dr. Barbara Frederickson of the University of North Carolina points to numerous health benefits of positivity as well:

- it increases levels of growth, bonding, and trust-related hormones

- diminishes an inflammatory response to stress and lowers stress-related hormones

- lowers blood pressure, reduces pain

- reduces susceptibility to colds and improves immune system functioning

- improves sleep

- decreases risk of diabetes and stroke

When I was coaching one MP (Member of Parliament in New Zealand), I was reminded of just how powerful this element of self-care is. Tom really took the positivity practise to heart and everyone who met him felt his optimistic energy as palpable warmth. He would listen to recordings of inspirational speakers while driving around Auckland to his many engagements. I am convinced that his focus on cultivating positivity, as well as assisting his health and endurance in a demanding role, was a key factor in his promotion to the ministerial position that he had been aiming for.

The 10 Types of Positivity

In her book *Positivity*, Frederickson identifies 10 different types of positivity:

Interest	Inspiration	Amusement	Joy	Gratitude
Love	Hope	Awe	Pride	Serenity

Which of the 10 types of positivity are your strengths? Which types would you like to enhance?

To remind yourself to cultivate these 10 types of positivity, here is a sentence to assist you:

In Amusement, Grace Hopped Proudly, Inspiring Joy and Love with her Awesome Serenade.

Gratitude

One kind of positivity that has received a good deal of research attention is gratitude. A grateful disposition predicts greater life satisfaction, optimism, and cooperation. Studies suggest gratitude also:

- lowers levels of envy

- lowers possessiveness

- lowers anxiety and depression

- decreases post-traumatic stress

- increases pro-social giving

- increases relationship satisfaction

- increases cooperation

Gratitude researchers have identified two key components of gratitude: affirmation of goodness and attribution (the source of goodness coming from outside ourselves). This attribution is a humble recognition of our interdependence. A grateful person accepts all life as a gift versus seeing it as a burden. A grateful person focuses on satisfaction instead of deprivation and sees through the lens of abundance instead of scarcity.

The Physiological Benefits of Gratitude

By focussing your attention on what you are grateful for, you literally transform your body chemistry and activate your positivity hormones (oxytocin, serotonin). Gratitude has been shown to increase dopamine (a reward-related neurotransmitter) and to increase (norepinephrine), a neurotransmitter related to alertness and brightness of mind. You can lift your spirits with this simple exercise: once or twice a week, spend a few minutes reflecting on and recording three things that you are grateful for as you review your week. Current research[1] suggests that doing this exercise daily is less effective than doing it just once or twice a week. This could be because in a daily practice you may be more apt to go through the motions as in a rote exercise instead of making the review more intentional as a weekly practice.

When Positivity and Gratitude Seem too Hard

It is important to admit that you may not always be able to easily access positive and grateful feelings. Pretending to feel happy when you are not is what I call a 'spiritual bypass.' If you want to avoid experiencing the heavier emotions by going straight into lightheartedness, you will likely feel a deep sense of inauthenticity. Rather, a healthier way to relate to your emotional life is to move in and through the layers of more challenging feelings. Through being willing to fully experience your uncomfortable emotions, your lightheartedness will surface in time. There can be real value in admitting and allowing the other more challenging feelings to be felt. Here is a process I call 'Heart Thawing' which you can apply when you feel numb or afraid or stuck and cannot seem to manage to access the positive, grateful state you would like. It is helpful to set aside about 15 minutes and ideally have a trusting partner or friend to listen without comment, to simply and silently witness you while you express yourself. (You can move through this process by yourself if you do not have someone available to listen, but a trusted supporter can make it more effective). An acronym to remember this process is, "From Bad, Mad, and Sad to Glad." The feelings you will move through are: Fear, Guilt, Shame, Anger, Sadness and Gladness. From (F is for fear), Bad (guilt or shame), Mad (anger, irritation, frustration) and Sad (hurt, grief, loneliness) to Glad (contentment, acceptance, joy, gratitude). Rather than jump straight to glad feelings, you move through the layers of fear, guilt, shame, anger, and sadness first. Begin the heart thawing process by saying everything you feel afraid of in a free-flowing, stream of consciousness style. Even though many of the fears may be irrational, just let them flow. For example, I feel afraid people will not like this book, I feel afraid of getting sick, I feel afraid my partner will leave me, I feel afraid that my son will move away, I feel afraid my back pain will not go away, I feel afraid and so on. After you have exhausted your list of fears and you cannot easily think of any more, move to expressing anything you feel guilty or ashamed about. I feel bad that . . .

Next, move to anger. I feel mad that . . . After you have expressed your anger, move to sadness. I feel sad that . . . After you have expressed your sadness, you will likely feel a release of tension in your body and you can authentically move into the lighter state of positivity and gratitude. I feel glad that . . .

Posture and Bearing

Your posture and bearing also greatly influence your vitality. They strongly affect your self-confidence as well as the way you are perceived by others and your ability to influence them.

In her 2015 book, *Presence: Bringing Your Boldest Self to Your Biggest Challenges*, Harvard social psychologist, Amy Cuddy, discusses the power of your physiology in producing confidence. If your parents ever told you, 'Sit up straight,' the science now suggests that their advice was well-placed and affects much more than just your appearance.

In Cuddy's research involving Harvard Business school students, her team discovered that after 15 minutes of what she calls 'power posing', students showed a 19% increase in testosterone (the confidence/assertiveness hormone) and a 25% decrease in cortisol (the stress hormone) in saliva tests. As I write this, one of Cuddy's co-researchers has expressed doubts about this research as she has been unable to duplicate the original results.

However, Cuddy cites numerous other studies besides her own which support the premise that there is a positive confidence effect from power posing. One client of mine who now works as a senior executive in Hong Kong swears by the 'Wonder Woman' pose in the toilet stall before her presentations (hands on hips, legs shoulder width apart). Also, in my experience as an actor, there is a real energetic effect in adopting a powerful pose to increase one's presence.

The Actor's Secret

Famous Russian acting teacher, Michael Chekhov, taught that the path to great acting was through physiology. His methods revolved around stimulating one's emotion through finding the gestures which evoked the thoughts and feelings of a character. In my first acting class at the Walnut Street Theatre in Philadelphia, we experimented with Chekhov's physiologically-based acting techniques. We were asked to adopt different postures and movements and then to notice which feelings arose in each posture. When I hunched over or squatted down to make myself feel smaller, I began to feel the inklings of sadness and loneliness. When I strutted around the room with large strides and open arms, I started to feel like a confident character.

University of Auckland Posture Study

One 2015 University of Auckland health psychology study concluded that adopting an upright posture in the face of stress can significantly impact on self-esteem, reduce negative mood and increase positive mood compared to a slumped posture. Furthermore, sitting upright during an interview/presentation situation was found to reduce self-focus and perceived threat.[2]

Identifying with the Power of Nature

I have found in my work with clients, however, that the advice, 'sit up straight' or, 'stand up straight' can cause overcompensating tension. I recommend imagining instead that you are a powerful being of nature, such as a tree, a mountain, or the sun. By identifying with and embodying images of these powerful symbols, you automatically improve your inner and outer stature which positively affects your mood and confidence without causing tension. One of my clients reported to me that he imagined himself as a kauri tree as he stepped up to the podium in front of a large audience. As he normally would stumble or stammer, he noted the positive difference. He felt a surge of confidence and stability in his speaking through identifying with this tree image. I have also had a client successfully use the image of the moon to strengthen her confidence during her presentations. I have personally found the image of the sun to create a feeling of strength and radiance when I am speaking with larger audiences. You can use different images depending on how you would like to feel. I recommend trying out various images to see which ones give you a sense of energy, presence, and confidence.

The Alexander Technique

Another powerful way to strengthen your posture and bearing and to release unnecessary tension is through a practice developed by the Australian actor, F. M. Alexander. The Alexander Technique is a method that works to enhance your movement and posture in everyday activities. It is a simple and practical method for improving ease and freedom of movement, balance, support, and coordination. Alexander was an actor who lost his voice. He consulted many doctors and they all told him the same thing. There was nothing physically wrong with his vocal apparatus. It was the way he was using his voice which was causing physical strain. In his determination to heal his voice, he discovered some principles which helped him to recover his full vocal function, as well as to launch his new career as a teacher of ease in performance.

Alexander Technique Pointers

One of the primary principles Alexander discovered is the importance of freeing the back of the neck from chronic tension. Holding tension in your neck so that the back of your head moves back and downward, your chin jutting forward, and your chest sinking, is a common habit which occurs under stress, or when performing repetitive work tasks like typing on a keypad while staring at your computer screen. By giving yourself the inner directives, 'Neck be free' and, 'Head move forward and up,' you can cultivate healthier movement and postural habits which support your most easeful performance of all your activities. Saying these directives to yourself, you will notice that your chest will naturally lift and your posture will be more aligned without you artificially puffing out your chest and trying to sit or stand up straight.

Overcoming Perfectionism and Self-Criticism

Are you familiar with the two common mental habits that thwart your vitality and your voice of leadership? The two habits I am referring to are perfectionism and self-criticism. I refer to these inner voices as 'Perfect Pat' and 'Critical Craig.' Perfect Pat might say things like, 'Your report is not quite detailed enough' or, 'You really should have prepared more for this presentation.'

Critical Craig might say, 'You are late again!' or, 'Your hair is a mess!' or, 'Why did you say that? . . . You should have said . . .' When Perfect Pat or Critical Craig start speaking, it is difficult to hear your own wisdom and to maintain your positivity. So, how do you transform these negative voices to support your presence, influence, and creative confidence? The answer lies in recognising that your perfectionist and your critic do want the best for you. They are well-meaning, but their harsh methods are misguided. They are under the illusion that if you just try harder you could be in control and perfect. They want you to do better, yet they actually can make you more afraid of failure and cause you to lose faith in yourself. They need strong guidance and redirection from you to be more effective.

Instead of 'whipping you into shape,' ask your critical inner voices to team up and take on a new job. Let them collaborate and give them a promotion, a new title. Call them your 'inner coach' or, as one of my clients prefers, your 'inner champion.' The role of your inner coach is to recognise that no one is perfect, and that speaking to you harshly can lead to depression and a hesitancy to act, to put yourself 'out there.' If the intention of Perfect Pat and Critical Craig is to help you to do better, ask them to be more encouraging. For example, the old way of perfectionism and criticism is to say, 'Why are you so afraid? There is nothing to be afraid of. Just get over it!' Instead, practise treating yourself like a supportive coach with affirming self-talk. Thoughts like, 'I admire your courage' or, 'I know you sincerely want to be of service,' are two examples. If you do recognise a mistake you have made, your inner coach can reassure you instead of beating you up. You could say to yourself, "Yes, there is an issue here, and I am here to help you to sort it. I am here to support you in learning and growing. It is only human to make mistakes. Let us correct our course and move on."

Pat realised that she had inherited her mother's intensity and had the tendency to be a perfectionist. As a CEO, Pat used to fire people she did not like. Her staff started to disrespect her and she could see some parallel tendencies in her relationship with her own mother. Pat began to disrespect her mother as her mother often spoke with a critical voice. Through becoming aware of this habit in herself, Pat realised her own need to switch off on a regular basis and to take some healthy breaks throughout the day. She realised she needed to lighten up her judgements of herself and others and become more tolerant. As she became more compassionate with herself, she noticed that her relationships with her staff and their performance began to improve as well.

An anti-perfectionism poem for your inspiration:

I would rather stumble a thousand times

Attempting to reach a goal,

Than to sit with the crowd in my weatherproof shroud

A shrivelled self-satisfied soul.

I would rather be doing and daring

All of my error filled days,

Than watching and waiting and dying,

Smug in my perfect ways.

I would rather wonder and blunder

Stumbling blindly ahead.

Than for safety's sake, lest I make a mistake

Be sure and secure – and dead.

Unknown Author

Play and Creativity

Another effective way to boost your vitality and creative confidence is through cultivating your sense of play. When I facilitate team-building sessions to cultivate authentic communication, I consistently find that play is the element that brings everyone together.

I worked with one team who were very guarded and shy in terms of expressing authentically with one another. The tension in the room at the beginning of our session was palpable. Shortly after we reviewed the researched benefits of play and initiated a few creative collaboration games, the whole atmosphere in the room changed. People were laughing, expressing themselves, taking risks and offering creative ideas. The vitality, energy, and excitement among the participants had significantly risen. When people are given permission and encouragement to play without performance pressure, they step into the zone of greater authenticity and creativity.

What is Play?

Play is a state of open-mindedness and non-judgement where there is no right or wrong. Play gives people permission to be free, opens up boundaries and invites more creative risk-taking. Play generates laughter, encourages inquiry, experimentation, and exploration. Collaboration and innovation thrive in a playful atmosphere of safety, non-criticism and democracy, where everyone's voice is heard. In addition, research by Dr. Robert Provine, neuroscientist and professor of psychology at the University of Maryland, suggests that laughter:

- decreases your blood pressure

- improves your immune function

- improves your sleep, and

- decreases depression and pain symptoms

Play Research

According to the National Institute for Play (NIFP), the practices that organisations need to be developing for their increasingly complex information work are those which infuse the state of play into their workers' attitudes. However, the NIFP has found that executives require sufficient immersion in the science of play before they understand and value it. The intellectual and scientific basis of play can provide the understanding and permission to give new play-based practices a go. Without a positive play ethic, the climate for innovation is talked about as important but not acted upon.

Wordplay

Here is an acronym to help you cultivate your most creative, innovative and playful self:

- **Presence (P)** – Develop your foundational capacity for innovation and play through cultivating awareness of the present moment. (see Mindfulness Exercises in this chapter)

- **Listening (L)** – (Receptivity, non-judgement, openness, interest). Remember to listen to yourself and others with an open-minded, accepting attitude. (For listening tips, see The Art of Conversation for Leaders, Key # 6).

- **Authenticity (A)** – (Contributing, trusting impulses, self-acceptance). (See Key # 6 for authentic communication tips).

- **Yes! (Y)** – (Non-resistance, going with the flow, accepting what is). There is a game you can play with a partner or alone which will build your capacity to go with the flow and experience the necessary non-resistance for your creativity to flourish. Think about an imaginary trip you are planning to take and brainstorm ideas for enjoyable activities. The only rule of the game is that you must

respond to each idea with 'Yes, but . . .' before adding
the next idea. Notice what happens to the creative energy
– it dies. In contrast, try the same exercise, and this time
the rule is you must begin every reply to each idea with
'Yes, and. . .' See how your energy builds and you free
up your imagination.

Play is Serious Business

Remember to '**Play**' to cultivate your collaboritude[3] (the
attitude necessary for innovation and collaboration) as well as
your vitality.

I used to think that being a leader meant being the serious one to
keep all those other unfocussed people on track. Now, I realise
that a leader sets the emotional tone for an organisation and that
fun is serious business.

A common focus for organisations these days is innovation.
Innovation is the process of coming up with new ideas, methods,
or products that create value. It is crucial to your success given
the accelerating pace of development in the world. If you want
to foster innovation, aim to establish an environment of play.
Innovation demands a willingness to explore and the freedom
to be able to fail often and fail fast. When we approach our
work as a playful adventure, we take the pressure off ourselves

and allow ourselves to act in an authentic and spontaneous way which leads to better results.

Following Your Flow

Hungarian psychologist Mihaly Csíkszentmihályi[4] recognised and named the psychological concept of flow, a highly focussed mental state. When I am focussed on my writing, I feel totally absorbed and time seems to fly by. All other distractions fade into the background. This state is called being 'in the flow.' What activity gives you the feeling of being in the flow? In his book *Flow: The Psychology of Optimal Experience*, Csíkszentmihályi outlines his theory that people are happiest when they are in a state of flow, a state of concentration or complete absorption with the activity at hand and the situation. It is a state in which you are so involved in an activity that nothing else seems to matter. The idea of flow is identical to the feeling of being in the zone. The state of flow is an optimal state of intrinsic motivation where you are fully immersed in what you are doing. It is a feeling of great absorption, engagement, fulfillment and skill, during which concerns like time, food and self are typically ignored. The more you can devote time to activities which activate a state of flow, the happier and more effective you will be.

Mindfulness

One popular and well-researched vitality strengthener is the practice of mindfulness. What exactly is mindfulness, how can it benefit you, and how can you develop it? Mindfulness is essentially the moment by moment non-judgmental awareness of your thoughts, feelings, body sensations and the surrounding environment. In over 3,000 studies, regular mindfulness practice has been shown to produce the following results:

- lowers anxiety, depression, and the stress response

- increases focus, concentration, memory, and cognitive control

- improves decision-making

- enhances pro-social, generous and optimistic behaviours

- improves sleep quality and general well-being

- increases clarity and quality strategic thinking

- reduces blood pressure

- decreases tiredness, aches and pains

Also, the brains of long-term mindfulness practitioners have been studied and they reveal a physical thickening or strengthening of the density of the grey matter in the hippocampus. The hippocampus is the area of the brain which controls learning and memory, attention, self-regulation, empathy, and compassion. It appears that due to the neuroplasticity or malleability of our brains, we can create new neural pathways which improve our cognitive and emotional capacities in a measurable way.

Companies like Google, Yahoo, Microsoft, and Facebook all have introduced mindfulness practice programmes in their organisations. When you look at the improvements that mindfulness is making, it is hard to imagine why you would not want to at least give it a try.

How Mindful are You?

One of the ways to assess your current level of mindfulness is to observe how often you are preoccupied with future or past events. Future planning is often critical for success, but it should not be at the expense of your mindful presence. When you are being mindfully present, you are in an optimum state to be most influential and effective. Ideally, you would reserve specific planning times in your day or in your week and spend most of your time focused on each activity happening in the moment.

Mindful Awareness-Building Exercise:

Here is a simple exercise to begin cultivating your presence as you go about your regular daily activities: at each of your meals and/or tea breaks (or whatever times are convenient to jog your memory), ask yourself these sensorial questions:

What am I seeing now? Notice the colours, shapes, objects, people, and so on.

Which sounds am I hearing now? Notice the whirr of a computer, traffic noises, a telephone ringing, and so on.

What sensations am I feeling now physically? Notice the chair beneath you, the temperature of the room, your feet on the floor, your breath, heartbeat, and so on.

What am I smelling or tasting now? Notice any smells or tastes, for example, coffee, toothpaste, breath mint, food, and so on.

What is my intuition telling me now? Notice what your 'sixth sense' is telling you.[5] Do you have a sense of 'rightness' or 'wrongness' about a particular situation, agreement, or plan?

Mindful Breathing: Calming the Monkey Mind

Another mindfulness practice is done from an upright, seated and still posture. As your mind has the natural tendency to jump around between various random thoughts (what is commonly referred to as 'monkey mind'), your breath can help you to calm down those monkeys.

Mindful Breathing Practice:

Adopt a seated position where you are on a firm surface with your feet flat on the floor and your back straight and place your hands on your knees.

With your next in-breath, turn over your right hand on your right knee, with your palm facing upwards. (Turn your palm up just a moment after you begin your in-breath. The breath always precedes the movement.)

Notice the natural pause at the end of your in-breath and allow your out-breath to begin to release naturally, as you turn your right hand over, palm down on your right knee.

Just after your next natural in-breath begins, turn your left palm upward on your left knee. Again, notice the slight pause at the top of your in-breath.

Turn your left hand over, palm down, on your left knee, just after your natural out-breath begins.

Continue with the exercise, turning up alternating palms with each in-breath, and down with each out-breath. With every out-breath, tap your knee as you exhale, adding an extra tap with each successive breath. Inhale, exhale (tapping your knee once with your right hand). Inhale, exhale (tap knee once with your left hand). Inhale, exhale (tap knee twice with your right hand). Inhale, exhale (tap knee twice with your left hand), and so on. Continue this pattern until you reach 10 taps on each knee. You will feel a sense of being more centred, alert, and grounded upon completion of this exercise.

Mindful Breathing Tips

Allow your breathing to be natural and reflexive rather than controlled. Relax your abdominal area and jaw as if you are about to yawn, lips closed with teeth slightly parted. Resist the temptation to control your breath. Just observe it. Allow your natural breathing reflex to do what it does naturally, ebbing and flowing like the ocean, naturally flowing into shore on the out-breath, pausing slightly before ebbing back into the sea on the in-breath. After your initial 10 breaths, if you want to continue your mindfulness practice, let your attention rest on your heart area and observe the subtle motion of expansion and release of your breath as your chest rises and falls. It can be helpful to inwardly say to yourself 'in' and 'out' as you experience the in-flow and out-flow of your breath.

Mindful Awareness Tips

If you find yourself being distracted by some physical or emotional pain, irritation or sensation, merely notice it and inwardly acknowledge it. For instance, if you notice your jaw feels tight, you note it silently, 'clenching, clenching' or 'holding, holding', simply acknowledging each experience as it arises. You may feel your back aching and inwardly you name the feeling. For example, you might note 'aching, aching, burning, burning, pulling, pulling, tightening, tightening,' What you will notice is that the dominant sensation continually shifts and changes, even if it is only in subtle ways. Let the focus of your attention rest on the dominant sensation, and when that sensation fades away or shifts, gently return your attention to the breath, inwardly noting with each in-breath and out-breath, 'in and out.' You might then, for instance, become aware of someone rustling a paper, so you inwardly note, 'rustling,

rustling.' As you continue this process, even for as little as five or 10 minutes, you will likely notice a sense of peace and clarity begin to arise. It is from this quietly attentive space called mindfulness, that your most inspired inner voice of leadership will whisper its insights to you.

Throughout the day, continue to be mindful by noticing yourself, the observer, the one who notices all your passing thoughts, feelings, and sensations. This is the one I call your Higher Self, with a capital 'S.' This observer is the source of your leadership presence. This is the Self that will guide you to appropriate activities and relationships which align with your purpose and natural energy. This is the Self which will lead you to greater vitality and a stronger voice of leadership.

Vital Social Connections

Do you realise the importance of your social network to your health and vitality? Research suggests that social exclusion or loneliness signals the same regions of the brain as physical pain. Social isolation has also been linked to increased inflammation in the body and difficulty sleeping.

Studies also indicate that online communication may especially benefit less extraverted individuals by giving them opportunities to provide support to others in a non-threatening environment, an experience that can in turn increase self-esteem and reduce depression.[6]

Your Wider Social Network

Surprisingly, research suggests that using Facebook can help to satisfy our need for connection. Researchers have referred to the looser ties formed in social media platforms as bridging relationships. Bridging relationships often involve weaker ties, but the breadth and diversity of these ties can expose us to new ideas and opportunities beyond what is available in our narrower inner circles. Studies have shown that job hunters who have a wide range of weak ties are more likely to be successful in their search than those who have stronger close relationships but a narrower range of relationships. In addition, people with a greater number of bridging relationships have been found to have a greater sense of connection to the wider community, a more open-minded attitude and a greater ability to garner support for a cause. Research indicates that people who have a broad range of different kinds of social roles tend to be healthier and more likely to attain professional success. Occupying varying roles across multiple domains can create a psychological safety net that protects us against threats to our sense of self-worth and in turn we are likely to suffer less stress.

Personal Friendships

Even though a wide social network supports us, we still need at least a couple of close friendships for our health and vitality. Close friendships provide our need for deeper connection and intimacy. Our closer friendships help us feel a sense of belonging and meet our needs to feel known and appreciated for who we are. Research suggests that our friends bring out the best in us in terms of our ability to know and understand another person's thoughts and feelings (empathic accuracy). Psychologist Dr. Elizabeth Page-Gould[7] and colleagues have shown that friendships across ethnic group boundaries can help reduce anxiety and potentially even improve physical health among people who tend to feel anxious in intergroup settings. The more we can switch our focus from maintaining our own self-image to remembering our genuine concern for our friends' well-being, the happier and healthier our friendships will be. Support in times of need is one of the major benefits of what researchers call bonding relationships. Bonding relationships may not give us the breadth and diversity of looser bridging-focussed ties but they give us the closeness and intimacy that social media cannot provide.

To boost your vitality and confidence, practise the following exercise

Reflect on and List your Accomplishments

In the evening before you go to sleep, write down and reflect on what you did well that day. You can keep it simple by using bullet points or write to your heart's content. By physically writing your self-acknowledgement, you are creating a concrete visual affirmation of your accomplishments. The goal of this exercise is to bring your focus and attention to at least three things you did well during the day. By doing this, you consciously nurture your sense of satisfaction with life. A common habit is to focus on all the incomplete items on the to-do list. However, focusing on what is undone can produce frustration and a continual sense of dissatisfaction with yourself, your capabilities, and your life. By writing about what you did well that day, you strengthen your creative confidence and develop a mind-set which activates a positive cycle of satisfaction. You cultivate your positive feelings about your accomplishments. These positive feelings serve to support your further confidence to pursue your goals and dreams. You support your self-image as someone who achieves successfully every day. You consequently feel more able to address unfinished tasks or to tackle new projects in the morning.

Key #4 Summary:

✓ Prioritise your self-care on all levels including your posture and bearing

✓ Cultivate the 10 types of positivity to thrive

✓ Give your inner critic a promotion to 'inner coach'

✓ Develop playfulness to enhance your creative confidence

✓ Nurture your social connections for greater health and influence

✓ Take time to practise mindfulness and activities which activate your flow state

✓ Reflect on and write about your accomplishments to build creative confidence

5

Visibility

I was jarred awake from a deep sleep by the ringing of my cellphone early one morning. I felt stunned when I heard my friend's alarmed voice expressing her shock to see a picture of herself with me and another friend of ours on Facebook. We had enjoyed a holiday reunion just the day before. As the photo was a simple straightforward picture of the three friends smiling, I did not anticipate that it would trigger such a strong response when I posted it. My friend was obviously distraught and told me that she guards her privacy carefully and asked me to take down the photo immediately. I felt surprised to hear her reaction, apologised and deleted the photo. This incident spurred me to reflect on just how challenging the issue of visibility can be for many people.

For the past 25 plus years I have been encouraged to become more visible as part of marketing my speaking and mentoring roles. I know from experience that visibility can frequently stretch you out of your comfort zone. When I was 30 years old and running my first 'Life Design' workshop in Boulder, Colorado, we did not have social media or even the internet yet, so I posted flyers on community notice boards. I remember going down to the local grocery store and cafe which was a popular community gathering spot with a large public bulletin board. I took my flyer in hand, along with my stapler and checked around me to make sure no one was looking. I quickly tacked my workshop announcement up on the board and promptly ran away to escape being seen.

A Visibility Lesson from the Acting World

Michael Gleason, the former director of the Los Angeles Musical Theatre Association, taught me a lesson about visibility which I will never forget. It is a powerful 'leadership presence' technique which I still continue to teach 25 years after first learning it. Michael told us aspiring young actors who attended his audition preparation workshop that he would teach us one secret that would "make our career". Although he listened to hundreds of hopeful actors who auditioned for him every year, he said he can tell if he wants to hire an actor "before he even opens his mouth". A good actor has talent. What is talent? It is energy. It is an energy that silently shouts with your whole being. What does it shout? . . .

"Look at me!" I want you to stop, look, and listen, because I have something important to say. I want to connect with you. I want the attention of every eye in the audience. A good actor does not begin speaking until he senses all eyes and ears are looking and listening.

This same tip applies to leaders and presenters. If you pause for a moment before you dive into a presentation, proposal, or interview answer, that moment of silence magnetises and hooks your audience. Remember that the reason you are wanting attention is to make sure your message is heard. You sincerely want to make a contribution. To do that, you need the full attention and engagement of your audience. Echoing Michael Gleason's advice, communication expert and my fellow University of Virginia alumnus, Nick Morgan, outlines the three components of charisma in his book *Trust Me: Four Steps to Authenticity and Charisma:*

- an awareness that people are looking at you

- expressiveness of a wide array of strong emotions, and

- an element of enjoyment of being the centre of attention

So, do not be afraid to step up into the limelight. As long as your intention is to serve your audience, you will not be perceived as a showoff. Your audience will be more apt to sit up and lean in to hear what you have to say if you 'own the stage.'

Stepping up, Speaking up, Standing out

Sarah had just transitioned from a small start-up company to a top executive position at one of the Fortune 50 companies in New Zealand. She wanted to be recognised and acknowledged for her contribution, yet she also realised she would need to first learn the unspoken rules of the new culture she was entering. She realised she would need to be politically aware and alert as there was already another woman who wanted her job. There were also some people in the organisation that were disgruntled that an outsider like Sarah was hired for the coveted senior executive position. As the leadership in her organisation was predominantly male, Sarah was finding it difficult to step up and stand out as her authentic self while still showing respect for the customs of the organisation. She now found herself in a place where shaking hands and wearing more formal attire was expected, whereas at the small start-up company she had come from, the culture was much more informal. She had stepped into the middle of a dominant old boy culture. She needed to learn to navigate this culture while at the same time challenging the organisation to try new ways of doing things. Before she took big risks in expressing her ideas, she first observed the way that people got noticed and recognised in the organisation. She then was able to acknowledge the norms of the group and express herself more intentionally by framing what she as doing in a way that people would be more apt to understand. People will be willing to be stretched and challenged as long as you let them know your intention and why you are taking them out of their comfort zone to try something new. The leaders in the organisation agreed that they needed to be more innovative, so when Sarah began to be more visible with her initiatives or 'experiments in innovation' as she called them, she was then able to get more attention, engagement, and cooperation from across the organisation.

Be Seen, be Heard and Connect with Stories

When I saw Kevin Roberts, Worldwide CEO of Saatchi and Saatchi speak at the National Speakers Association of Australia's conference several years ago, he said something that stuck: What your customers want more than anything else is a sense of intimacy, a personal connection with you and your product or service. One powerful way to nurture that sense of intimacy is through storytelling. To get noticed, to build connections and to be more influential, it is helpful to hone your personal storytelling skills. Storytelling can transform your communication from an ordinary exchange to a highly engaging interaction with memorable impact. Sharing personal stories which are relevant and emotionally connected to others' concerns can build trust and connection, create a sense of shared values, and motivate and inspire action. Here are six pointers to keep in mind when telling a story as part of a presentation or a conversation:

1. **Link your story to the audience to help them connect with it** – Example: Have you ever left a job to start a new career or business? You know that sense of excitement and anticipation you get when you are starting a new chapter of your life? Well, when I was 25, I left my corporate job and decided to pursue a career as a professional actress. .

2. **Change your voice and gestures to represent the different characters in your story** – Example: You know how your parents have a way of pushing your buttons? Well, last year

I went back to the States to visit my mother, and we went shopping. I am trying on swimsuits in the dressing room, and she says (I imitate her voice and facial expressions), 'Honey, isn't that new boyfriend of yours a personal trainer? . . .Can't he doooo something about that middle?' By mimicking the voices in an actual conversation, you add animating colour and humour to your story. Speaking in a voice like my mother was much more memorable and vivid than if I had merely reported what she said like this: 'My mother told me she thought that I should do some personal training to reduce my waistline'.

3. **Tell your story as if it is happening now** – Example: I finally summoned the courage to get on the phone and say to the CEO, "I must apologise as I am running late and will not make it to our session this morning." This is not welcome news from his time management coach!

4. **Invest yourself emotionally in your story** – Be 60% involved in the emotion of the story while you the other 40% of your attention keeps track of your story as a director. If you put yourself into your story emotionally, it is much more engaging for your audience. However, as a storyteller, you want to make sure that you do not

lose the objective perspective of a director by getting too self-absorbed in the emotion. Maintaining the objectivity of a director while still feeling and conveying the emotion of your story takes practice.

5. **After you have told your story, bring home the point that relates to your audience** – Example: The next time someone criticises you, just remember that they are looking at you through the lens of their own beliefs and values. You do not have to accept their comments as relevant to you. Hold fast to your own sense of truth and integrity.

6. **Tell stories where you are the 'fool' or the 'failure'** – When you courageously reveal your vulnerability, you connect with the audience's vulnerability and they are grateful for the sense of intimacy you create with them. They experience your pain with you and can relate to you more closely as it stirs their empathy. They realise they are not the only ones who have done foolish things or made mistakes. For example, one story which always seems to create a collective empathic response from my audience is my embarrassing fiasco of oversleeping and missing the time management seminar I was scheduled to facilitate for a group of senior executives. I balance these

self-deprecating stories by sprinkling them with a few stories of success, but I give the failure themes precedence as they create the most humour, take the most courage, and produce the greatest connection with the audience.

In short, the heart of great stories is conflict. They are all about disruptions to status quo and have turns or surprises in them. They create suspense and reinforce important social values. The characters in your stories should always learn a lesson which relates to the audience's life in some way. Make sure your stories are relevant and frame them so that the point you are making is clear to your audience. Remember, the stories should always ultimately be told for the benefit of your listener. To help you reflect on stories from your own life which you could consider telling in a meaningful way, I suggest you reflect on each decade of your life and make some notes. Think back to your first 10 years of life. Record memories of incidents that happened to you and then think of what lessons the incident taught you and meaning you could extrapolate for others. Then reflect on stories from age 10-20, 20-30 and so on up until your current age. You can keep a file of these stories along with the points you want to make and keep it as a reference for you as needed. Look for opportunities to weave these stories into your conversations and presentations to make them more compelling.

Visibility Through Public Speaking

Public speaking is a powerful way to draw people in to pay attention to your message and to have a memorable impact. An influential presentation or conversation should convince your audience that it is worth their while to listen. You want to make your audience feel that what you have to say is important enough for them to be willing to allow you to take up their precious time and energy. You also want to relate to them as a friend – a guide on the side versus a sage on the stage.

Below is a seven-step guide followed by an example to help you create a presentation which will have an impact on your audience and create more visibility for you and your project or mission. The seven steps are first described and then followed by a specific example:

1. **Opening question or impactful statement** – This is your first sentence which grabs your audience's attention and engages their curiosity. Your initial words will draw them in to listen to the rest of what you have to say.

2. **Outcome statement** – This statement clearly tells your audience what you want them to feel, think, or do as a result of your talk.

3. **Frame** – The frame is the context for why you feel this topic is important, why it is urgent or particularly relevant today, and why you are specifically presenting on this topic. (Why this? Why now? Why me?[1])

4. **Problem/Consequences** – Take time to elaborate on the relevant and current issue or problem for which you are promoting a solution. You will more deeply explore what is currently happening in the organisation/ the market/ the world and the pressing issues or challenges your audience faces.

5. **Solution** – This comes near the end of your presentation, after you have built the tension by highlighting the problem and consequences they are facing, your audience will be ready and eager to hear your specific ideas and tools you are offering as a solution to their particular issue or problem.

6. **Promotional piece and call to action** – Do this before you close. This is the time to announce any special events or offers and to inspire your audience to take action and to activate the solutions you are presenting.

7. **Summary and Close**

Here is an example to give you a clear picture of the seven-step process to influential speaking:

1. **Opening** – Do you suffer from C.D.D.? (pause and look around for audience response). You have heard of C.D.D., yes? . . . (see questioning looks . . . pause). Most people suffer from it. You are not alone . . . C.D.D. . . . . Confidence-Deficit-Disorder (I now have their attention and a bit of a chuckle).

2. **Outcome** – Well, my hope is that today you will get some relief from any symptoms of C.D.D. and you walk away feeling inspired, empowered, and committed to expressing your voice of leadership.

3. **Frame** – What is your voice of leadership and why is it so important? Your voice of leadership is that voice you speak with that is clear, confident, and connected to your highest aspirations. You feel 'in the flow' and 'on top of your game.' Your success as a speaker or presenter is mostly determined by your 'inner state' or energy, so it is critical that you learn some practical tools to keep you on a positive track.

4. **Problem/Consequences** – So many people today are not connected to their voice of leadership . . . how do we know this? A recent study of 23,000 employees (as cited in Stephen R. Covey's book *The 8th Habit*) shows that only 15% of

employees feel they work in a high trust environment and only 17% of employees feel they have open communication at work. What does this tell us? The message is that many people are not speaking up with their voice of leadership. They are not being clear, confident, and connected with their purpose. Another study of 10,000 executives cited in American Salesman Magazine suggests that most of us are afraid of public speaking.

If you lack confidence in speaking, you lack the ability to build trust and connection with your audience. If you are in business, this lack of confidence can result in lost sales, reduced client loyalty, missed promotions, and a poorer bottom line.

Your personal relationships as well as your mental and emotional health can be compromised by an inability to be clear, confident, and connected in your communication.

5. **Solution** – So how do you develop your voice of leadership and step into greater confidence?

Here is the point where I bring in some tools according to the needs of the audience. These are selected from some of the tools included in this book: The three R's of vocal projection, the five dynamics of expressive speaking, tongue twisters to practice clear articulation, seven steps to crafting a presentation, seven steps to powerful presence, and so on.

6. **Promotional piece and call to action** – So, if you are committed to expressing your voice of leadership, projecting more confidence, attracting more clients, and enjoying yourself and others more when you speak, I encourage you to come to my next course: 'Express Your Voice of Leadership' on X date or to see me regarding a private mentoring program or an in-house course for your staff.

7. **Summary and Close** – We have talked about how this lack of confidence is an epidemic and very detrimental to your career in any leadership position. We have outlined specific tools you can use to start developing your voice of leadership. Now, I would like to leave you with some inspirational words from the famous motivation and leadership guru, Dale Carnegie:

"Only the prepared speaker deserves to be confident. Do the thing you fear to do and keep on doing it – that is the quickest and surest way ever yet discovered to conquer fear. If you want to conquer fear, do not sit home and think about it. Go out and get busy."

Go forward now with confidence and courage to express your Voice of Leadership!

Remember to craft your message with these seven steps and you will be more effective in getting seen, heard and eliciting a positive response from your listeners.

Your Appearance and Visibility

"The body is the shell of the soul, and dress the husk of that shell; but the husk often tells what the kernel is."
Anonymous

According to 2011 research by Harvard Medical School and Massachusetts General Hospital, people assess your competence and trustworthiness in a quarter of a second (250 milliseconds) based solely on how you look!

Although you cannot control others' judgements, you can increase your positive visibility. Some of the factors you can control to a large degree include being polished and groomed, being physically fit, having an enthusiastic demeanor and wearing simple, stylish clothes that position you for your next job. Do not underestimate the importance of your appearance in creating your Executive Presence.

Executive Appearance Tips:

Take notice of the colours you wear. Darker colours convey a stronger impression than lighter ones. Wear rich colours to portray authority. Consider getting professional advice on the colours that best suit your skin complexion.

Professional grooming and polish is important to gain respect and make a positive impression in the workplace. The way you groom yourself creates an impression (rightly or wrongly), of the care you will take with clients, colleagues, and your work in general. A women's polish includes tasteful accessories, manicured nails and a flattering hairstyle. A man's polish includes clean nails, shiny shoes, a clean shave or neatly trimmed or shaved facial hair (2012, Centre for Talent Innovation, CTI survey). For both women and men, simple, stylish clothes that position you for the next job are part of your polish.

Taking care of yourself through a balanced diet and regular exercise creates a healthy vehicle for your professional self-expression. You do not need to be a certain weight, to be extremely muscled or to have a model body to feel fit. Caring for your fitness needs in a moderate way will help you exude an energetic presence of vitality. Feeling fit will support your confidence and well-being.

The Art of 'Owning the Space'

Tom became aware through our mentoring process of his tendency to fill any silent space with talking. He realised that he felt some anxiety in meeting with senior executives and had the habit of what he called 'jibber jabber' as a way to deal with his uneasiness. A key skill of 'gravitas' or leadership presence is the ability to hold silence.

Gravitas-Boosting Tip:

Here is a tip to boost your gravitas when you find yourself in a challenging communication situation:

Exhale fully, and then inhale slowly and deeply while you repeat your voice of leadership statement to yourself: For example, "I am clear and confident, and I have a strong leadership presence." Sit up or stand up with a relaxed but erect posture, and continue to breathe deeply and slowly while you listen to others, sit in silence, or naturally contribute to the conversation in a relaxed way.

Seven Steps to Powerful Presence

Through my own experimentation with finding ways to capture and engage attention as well as to feel more confident when presenting myself, I created seven reminders in the form of an easy-to-remember phrase. Many of my clients now also refer to this phrase when they want to boost their visibility and confidence. These seven steps have been blended and integrated from my professional acting experience, my study and practice of mindfulness meditation, and my involvement with personal development and leadership courses.

I remember the seven steps through the sentence: Look at me, as I breathe in nature, sensing what is present, embracing everyone, focusing on service, in body, heart, mind, and spirit.

Experiment with these steps for yourself and find out what works for you.

1. **Look at Me** – It is important to pause and wait a moment before launching into your presentation. By standing and looking around the room for a moment to connect with your audience in silence, you build up the suspense and signal that an important communication is about to take place. Taking a brief pause before you begin enhances your own presence, as well as your connection with your audience.

Also, in her latest research on eye contact, Australian social cognitive neuroscience researcher, Dr. Fiona Kerr, says, "When your retina aligns with mine, the right hemisphere of my brain will align with your right hemisphere, the creative, intuitive, relational side. Apparently, eye contact also stimulates oxytocin and serotonin production. These hormones help to boost the immune system and endocrine system, which produce hormones and helps regulate mood, growth and development".

2. **As I Breathe** – Breathing deeply and slowly while you are getting ready to present can have numerous positive effects. You lower the level of stress hormones in your body, such as cortisol and adrenalin, which helps you stay grounded and connected with your audience.

3. **In Nature** – Nature is a powerful teacher of 'presence.' The sun, the ocean, a tree, a lake, and so on are all powerfully 'present' without needing to prove themselves. They are all full of the life force which connects everything and everyone. If you find yourself feeling nervous before a presentation or conversation, imagine that you are actually embodying the quality of whatever natural symbol represents power to you. For instance, if you need more energy, you could imagine the sun radiating out from your centre. If you need more

calmness, you could imagine being surrounded by a deep, still lake or standing tall like a strong tree or a mountain.

4. **Sensing what is Present** – To calm a spinning mind prior to or during a presentation, you can focus on any of your five senses to get you 'out of your head' and into your body. Doing simple tasks like seeing and counting the chairs in the room or noting the various sounds in the room can be enormously helpful. Feel your feet on the ground; feel the temperature of the room. Are there any smells you notice?

5. **Embracing Everyone** – Keep in mind all you have in common with your audience. We are all fellow travellers on this adventure called life. We are all travellers with similar needs. We all need to sleep, eat, love and be loved. We were all born and we will all die one day. We have all experienced the vast array of human emotions: fear, anger, sadness, joy, embarrassment. In short, we are first and foremost fellow human beings. When you embrace everyone with this perspective, including yourself, you will have more confidence, compassion, and presence. You will lessen your sense of separation, which is ultimately the source of all fear and nervousness.

6. **Focussing on Service** – Focus on what your audience needs, and how you can help them instead of your own self-consciousness. What are their interests? Why do they want to listen to you? How can you help them? By focussing on these questions, you more easily lose your self-consciousness and more fully engage your audience.

7. **In Body, Heart, Mind & Spirit** – When you address all four levels of human experience (physical, emotional, mental, and spiritual), you have a greater chance of connecting with your audience.

   Body (Physical) – Consider what you can have your audience do physically to engage with your presentation. Do you want to ask them to raise their hands to answer a question or to share their answers with a neighbour? Perhaps you want them to write something down to remember. I find that getting my audience up on their feet and interacting with specific voice exercises, for instance, gets them laughing and increases their energy and engagement. All of my keynote talks include an element of physical interaction.

   Heart (Emotional) – Which stories can you tell which will connect with your audience's emotional experience? For example, do you have any embarrassing mishaps which happened at work or at home which have taught you valuable lessons in an area applicable and relevant to your audience?

Mind (Mental) – Is your presentation well-structured, logical, and with plenty of support material? Have you included statistics, facts, and easy-to-remember action steps like 'The Three R's of projecting your voice'?

Spirit (Bigger Picture) – What inspirational elements will you include in your presentation, such as uplifting or thought-provoking poems, quotes, or metaphors? Have you included any metaphors to help your audience grasp the 'bigger picture' of your message?

Your Voice of Leadership Elevator Pitch

Self-promotion can be uncomfortable and in the Māori culture of Aotearoa / New Zealand, humility is paramount. There is a Maori proverb (whakataukī) which says, "Kāore te kumara e kōrero ana mo tōna ake reka". The English translation is: 'The kumara never speaks of its own sweetness.' (A kumara is a sweet potato to those in the northern hemisphere). However, when you need to explain what you do, it is best to be prepared rather than to waffle. When you are asked to introduce yourself in a professional networking setting, it is helpful to have a technique to get your message across succinctly and powerfully. This technique is commonly known as an elevator pitch. The elevator pitch is a short laser-focussed way to communicate what you do in the time it would take for you to share a ride with someone in an elevator for sixty seconds. You can also use an elevator pitch on social media sites where you now have the opportunity to be more visible than ever before. Today, you are competing with noise from increasingly numerous channels, so it is vital to communicate succinctly and with a strong authentic voice to cut through the din. In the age of information overload, we have to be more masterful at getting our messages across in a focussed way without wasting time.

Answer these five questions to design your own 60-second pitch which you can use the next time you are asked, whether in person or on-line – 'What do you do?'

Crafting Your Elevator Pitch

1. Who do you help?

2. What problem do you solve for them?

3. What benefit do they receive?

4. How do you solve the problem?

5. What is your call to action?

Instead of giving the answers to these five questions as a monologue, aim to reply conversationally. Here is an example of my voice of leadership elevator pitch which I adapt as needed in various networking situations.

"You know how entrepreneurs and business leaders often need to present and promote themselves and their businesses, and they may not feel so confident in doing that? (Answers questions #1 and #2 – Who do you help and what problem do they have?)

Well, I help them express what I call their voice of leadership so they can be clear, confident, and connected to their purpose and their listeners when they communicate.

Then, they are more able to engage and inspire others when they deliver their message. As a result, they can attract more business and be more successful (Answers question #3 – What benefit do they receive from working with you?)

I work with clients in a number of ways:

I offer public and in-house courses, interactive keynote presentations, private or group mentoring sessions, and I also wrote a book which teaches 'the six keys to presence, influence, and creative confidence (Answers question #4 - How do you solve the problem?)

Would you be interested in receiving my free monthly newsletter with updated event information?" (If yes, ask for business card). (This kind of question, #5 is your call to action).

The above pitch is 145 words – I recommend keeping your pitch short and sweet – up to 150 words.

Always remember that while it is important to have your pitch ready when you are networking, it is even more important to show interest in others by asking questions of them and hearing about their business. People tend to like and want to do business with those who express an interest in them. If you listen, ask questions, and collect cards rather than give your elevator pitch, you can still be equally, if not more effective. People love others who listen to them. You can follow up afterwards by phone or email with those who could benefit from your service, skill, or product.

Key # 5 Summary:

✓ Remember your intentional moment of silence to engage attention before speaking

✓ Storytelling is a powerful way to engage your audience if you make references to how the story applies to them

✓ Remember the Seven Steps to Crafting a Persuasive Presentation:

- Opening
- Outcome
- Frame
- Problem/consequence
- Solution
- Call to action
- Summary/close

✓ Remember the Seven Keys to Powerful Presence: Look at me, as I breathe, in nature, sensing what is present, embracing everyone, focusing on service, in body, heart, mind and spirit

✓ Your 60-second elevator pitch is a quick and focussed way to make a memorable impression

Veneration

Imagine you are getting ready to initiate a courageous conversation or to give a challenging presentation, whichever situation seems more daring to you. You are worried that you are not prepared enough or quick enough on your feet. You feel you are not polished enough, smart enough or dressed professionally enough. You feel anxious that others will find out the truth that you are not really worthy of being heard, that your conversation or presentation is not worthy of their full attention. Does any of this sound familiar to you? If so, you are not alone. Many of my clients have reported these common fears.

What are the situations in your life where you fear speaking up? Do you feel frustrated, for example, when someone is dominating the conversation and not interested in what you have to say? If your answer is yes, again you are not unusual. Most of us were not taught assertive speaking skills, nor did we have exemplary role models of healthy communication. I remember hearing advice from my mother that if I did not like something, rather than say so, I should say that it was 'interesting.' I was not taught to pay attention to my intuition.

I have ignored my intuition in the past to my financial peril. This resulted in one situation where I ignored my inner voice warning me not to lend $80,000 to a particular businessman in Boulder, Colorado. My intuition told me that this man was not trustworthy, even though on paper the loan appeared to be a good investment. Operating solely from logic and too much in a hurry to pay attention to my intuition, I signed the loan agreement despite my secret misgivings. The business I invested in ended up failing, the businessman defaulted on the loan, and my husband and I lost $80,000 in the end. Your intuition is there for a reason. Learn to cultivate it or ignore it at your peril.

Veneration is the key I was missing at that time to carefully listen to my heart and speak my mind. Veneration is an attitude of deep respect which honours the dignity of every person, including your own. It is that special ingredient which helps people to feel cared for and valued, with a sense of safety and permission for full self-expression. When you set the tone of veneration in your life and work, you can expect others to be more open and direct with you. This trusting environment is foundational to enjoyment, productivity, and creative collaboration both at work and at home.

Start with Self-Compassion (Self-Veneration)

A good place to begin practising veneration is in your relationship with yourself. With patience, persistence, and practice, you can replace habitual self-criticism and self-denial with habitual self-respect. Self-compassion is the key. Pioneering research by Dr. Kristin Neff,[1] Associate Professor at the University of Texas, has shown that self-compassion is correlated with:

- lower levels of anxiety and depression
- lower levels of stress hormones
- less rumination (overthinking or repetitive negative thinking)

- less perfectionism and fear of failure

- better coping with stress

- greater willingness to validate negative emotions versus suppressing them

- wisdom, happiness and optimism

- curiosity, exploration, and initiative

- emotional intelligence and improved relationships

Neff's research suggests that self-compassion is a much more effective self-motivational strategy than self-criticism. Self-criticism gives us the illusion of control, the illusion that 'if I just try harder, I could be perfect.' Self-compassion on the other hand, is not passive complacency. There is an interesting paradox that when you accept yourself just as you are, you are less defensive and can then be open to change more easily.

ACT with Self-Compassion (Self-Veneration)

Here is a simple three-step process to strengthen your self-compassion. This process was inspired by Neff's research as well as my own experience in experimenting with various therapeutic approaches to self-compassion. I have used this process successfully with myself as well as with my mentoring clients, and I encourage you to test it out for yourself.

When you are in a situation that is painful or uncomfortable, and you are tempted to criticise yourself, remember the word 'ACT' to remind yourself to act with self-compassion.

Three Steps to Self-Compassion:

A   **'Acknowledge'** – Acknowledge the pain or discomfort you are feeling.

C   **'Common'** – Realise that what you are feeling is a common human experience. You are not alone or unusual.

T   **'Treat'** – Treat yourself with kindness. Find a physical gesture that is appropriate in your present environment and company, to express compassion for yourself. This gesture could be a stroking of your cheek, a gentle resting of your hand over your heart, or any physical gesture which feels reassuring and supportive to you. This may initially feel strange if you are not used to treating yourself with affection. However, with practice you will get more comfortable with physical self-compassionate gestures.

When you make a habit of taking these three steps to self-compassion (ACT), you build up your self-kindness muscle and feel an energetic softening in your body and emotions. As you master treating yourself with compassion, you create more inner peace, presence and balance. You become a much stronger agent of change in terms of creating a culture of veneration at work and at home. Consider yourself a cultural change agent, spreading the attitude of veneration wherever you go.

"If you want others to be happy, practice compassion.
If you want to be happy, practice compassion."

Dalai Lama

Feelings and Needs Literacy

Do you often hesitate to express your feelings or judge them as unacceptable, inappropriate, or embarrassing? You may feel that you are exercising discernment in being silent. However, if you are holding back due to fear, you may be lacking veneration for your own right to speak and be heard. Strengthening your emotional literacy will support you to summon the courage to speak up when necessary.

In one of the first acting classes I attended, my teacher, Gordon Phillips of the Wilma Theatre in Philadelphia, taught us that there were only four basic categories of emotions: Mad, Sad, Glad, and Afraid. He taught us to identify which emotion or combination of emotions we were feeling to better express ourselves as actors. When I was a guest teacher for Kedgley Intermediate School here in Auckland a few years ago, I was shown a workbook from the Hauora Health Curriculum which included 'Bad' as a fifth category of emotions. (Although the word 'bad' can describe a self-judgement or a state of illness, I have found it useful for some to identify certain emotional states.)

Ask yourself the following question whenever you notice an emotion arise: "Which one of the five major emotions does this feel like – Mad, Bad, Sad, Glad, or Afraid? Or, is this sensation a combination of these emotions?" Refer to the common feelings list in Appendix II to increase your emotional vocabulary and your ability to communicate your feelings more clearly.

After you identify which of the five major emotions you are feeling, ask yourself, "What is the message that this feeling is telling me about what I am wanting, needing, or valuing right now?" For instance, if you are feeling mad, do you want more acknowledgement, respect or consideration? Ask yourself if you can do something differently or think about something differently to get that need met. For example, can you appreciate yourself more to get your need for acknowledgement met? Can you shift your attitude to be gentler on yourself in order to get your need for self-compassion met? Can you ask someone else for acknowledgement, consideration and/or for listening and feedback? For a list of common needs, refer to Appendix III.

The Messages of Feelings
Let us look at some of the common messages behind the five major feelings:

Mad   "Something is not right." A value you hold dear has been violated. You need to protect or restore something.

Bad   "I didn't uphold my own standards or act in line with my own self-image." You need to either change your standards or change your actions to align with your values.

Sad   "I have lost something." What do you need to let go of or what or who do you need to say goodbye to and mourn?

Glad "Some important need, want or value has just been satisfied."

Afraid "Get prepared, be alert, or protect yourself."

When challenging feelings arise, remember that any reaction is an expression of unmet needs.[2] If you can hear anger and hurt in this light, you will be more likely to respond in a healthy and effective way. If you can assist others to get those needs or values satisfied, you will have more successful, influential interactions. When you improve your ability to recognise and to share your feelings, you improve your ability to connect and to collaborate with others. When people understand your feelings, needs, and values, they are more apt to respond positively to your requests.

Assertiveness (Veneration for your needs and values)

Do you often hold back your ideas or feelings during a meeting, due either to self-consciousness, hierarchy reasons, or fear of offending someone? Then afterwards, you think of all the things you should have said? Speaking up assertively when you have a genuine need is critical to developing a strong voice of leadership. However, we are not generally taught this essential communication skill in school. Assertiveness is essential to developing a trusting relationship with yourself and others. It could even mean the difference between life and death in certain circumstances.

Let us consider the plane crash incidents cited by Malcolm Gladwell in his book *Outliers: The Story of Success*.[3] Gladwell relates three extreme examples of how failure to communicate assertively cost hundreds of people their lives. All three of the plane crashes Gladwell describes could have been prevented by assertive communication. In each of these tragic situations, hesitancy to speak up was the fatal error. One of the incidents involved a co-pilot feeling wary of icy conditions and ice on the plane's wings before takeoff. He did not directly speak up to the captain when he sensed the problem. His silence resulted in the plane crashing in the Potomac River in Washington, D.C. shortly after takeoff, killing 80 people on board. Another incident involved a co-pilot being afraid to speak up about the dangerously low level of fuel in the aircraft. Because he failed to speak up when he initially registered the problem, the plane ran out of fuel in midair and tragically crashed. The third incident involved a similar hesitancy to speak up, and another plane crashed into a mountain which was masked by cloud cover.

Thankfully, in the past 15 years, commercial airlines have treated non-assertiveness seriously and have instituted new training programmes specifically designed to teach co-pilots to speak up and challenge a pilot when they first become aware of a potential danger. They are required to seize control of the plane if the captain ignores them. Airlines now typically split the flying duties equally between the captain and co-pilot, to account for the tendency to avoid speaking up to a superior. Research has shown that crashes are far more likely when the captain is in the 'flying seat.' Planes are safer when the less experienced co-pilot is flying, because it means that the second in command gets to sit in the control seat and so assumes more authority to speak up.

Communication with Veneration

Although hierarchies of command can strongly hinder your ability to speak up assertively, you can still benefit by developing assertive communication skills no matter what organisational structure you encounter. Becoming a master communicator full of veneration is one of the key tasks of a leader. In the 2015 book, *Wayfinding Leadership: Ground-breaking Wisdom for Developing Leaders*[4], New Zealand-based authors Chellie Spiller, Hoturoa Barclay-Kerr, and John Panoho quote a powerful description of the authentic voice of leadership. This poetic summary of the attributes of leadership (rangatiratanga) from a Māori perspective, highlights communication and veneration as paramount. This quote is by Bishop Manuhia Bennett, as presented by Selwyn Katene, Professor and Director of the Global Centre for Indigenous Leadership:

Te kai o te rangatira, he kōrero (The food of a leader is talk)

Te tohu o te rangatira, he manaaki (The sign of a leader is generosity)

Te mahi o te rangatira, he whakatira i te iwi (The work of a leader is to unite people)

When I worked with a group of volunteers to help with an event organised by the Māori iwi (tribe) Ngāti Whātua and Auckland Council, we were given the job of helping to keep the festival grounds free from rubbish. Ngāti Whātua's policy is to aim for zero-waste. The organiser said that although our team would be picking up and sorting through rubbish, this job would whakamana (give respect to) the coordinators of this important function. In the Māori way of leadership, mutual respect, supporting the mana or dignity of people is considered an essential leadership skill.

Unfortunately, veneration is not always supported in an organisation's culture. With the performance pressures created by deadlines, budgets, and other issues related to business survival in a competitive climate, it is an act of courageous cultural change to speak your mind. In one organisation I recently worked with, the culture was such that many normally confident people were hesitant to speak up to their superiors. Many of the young aspiring leaders felt doubtful, anxious, and hopeless that their voices would be heard and treated with respect. They felt that a few of the leaders were not interested in hearing their opinions and just wanted them to follow orders. The team wanted acknowledgement and appreciation for their contributions and encouragement and support in their continuing efforts on behalf of the organisation. Fortunately, John, one of the senior leaders, was receptive to my feedback about why many of his staff were not speaking up in meetings as he wanted them to do. John took their concerns seriously and began scheduling regular meetings with the staff to hear their concerns and to discuss their ideas. I applaud John's efforts and his commitment to help shift the organisation's culture. I worked with his team on developing their voice of leadership and gave them five specific steps to support their growing courage to create an environment of veneration.

Five Steps to Assertive Speaking

Here is a process to support your courage to speak with the veneration and skill of a leader so that people will be more apt to listen to what you have to say, rather than defend. The process is especially useful when you are in a highly-charged situation. I recommend you first practise these steps with trusted friends and colleagues in an emotionally-supportive environment before practising them in real life situations. You can also practise these steps on your own as a way to clarify what you need and how you want to communicate with others. Over time, this process will help you to successfully collaborate, create harmony in your relationships and transform frustration into constructive action.

You can use these steps in the moment when difficult situations arise and as you practise them, the steps will start to become second nature. You can also use this process in less spontaneous situations, for example when responding to an email. It is also effective to work through the steps in writing before attempting to communicate with others. Writing the process will assist with your clarity and objectivity. You will be amazed at how the process will positively alter the way you respond. To begin the five steps to assertive speaking, remember the phrase:

'Beware Or Feelings Will Really Rule! (BFWRR)'

Step 1: B/O is for Behaviour/Observation

Step 2: F is for Feelings

Step 3: W is for Wants

Step 4: R is for Request

Step 5: R is for Result

Consider a typical situation in which the impulse to speak up arises. Picture yourself sitting in a team meeting. Imagine the person leading the meeting is dominating the 'air time' and not allowing you or others space to respond or contribute.

> **Step 1: Behaviour/Observation** – Notice the behaviour that is triggering your frustration. Summon your courage to share your observation about the specific behaviour of others or the facts you observe.
>
> You notice that Mike, the convenor, is still talking when there are only a few minutes left in the scheduled meeting time. You notice that others, including yourself, have not been asked for their input into the conversation.

Step 2: Feeling – Notice the sensation you have in your body in response to that behavior. Observe and inwardly note it to yourself – for example, you feel a tightness in your chest which you associate with feeling frustrated. (For a comprehensive list of common feelings to increase your emotional literacy, see Appendix II).

Step 3: Want – Ask yourself what you are wanting, needing or valuing in this moment. Any uncomfortable feeling is a sign that something you want, need, or value is not present in your current situation – for example, I want to make sure that we each get a chance to share our ideas before we leave here today. (For a comprehensive list of common wants, needs, and values, see Appendix III).

Step 4: Request – Share your observation, feelings and wants, needs, and/or values and make a specific request. "Pardon me, Mike, I'm feeling concerned (no blame – you are simply owning your own feelings) that we only have a few minutes left in our meeting and we have yet to hear from everyone.

"I want to make sure that we all get a chance to add our ideas before we leave here today. Can we check in with everyone to see if anyone else has something to contribute?"

Step 5: Result – Acknowledge the result of your request. If you got a positive response to your request, enjoy the satisfaction of having spoken up and been effective. Acknowledge yourself for your courage. If someone ignores or denies your request, you can start the five-step process again by acknowledging/observing this denial, your feelings and underlying wants. If someone continually denies your requests, you have an opportunity to practice self-compassion and you may choose to remove yourself from that situation. Only you will know the right move for you.

If you are pressed for time, you can work through a short form of this process by bringing to mind the acronym BFWRR. Ask yourself, "What are the behaviours/observations, the feelings, the wants/needs, and the requests of both myself and the other person?" By practising this BFWRR process, you are more likely to get a positive response than if you either hold in your anger in resentment or blow up at the person in frustration. This process takes long-term practice, so be easy on yourself as you are trying it out. As you get familiar with the five steps, you will feel more confident asserting yourself.

Practising Empathy (Veneration for the wants, needs, and values of yourself and others)

The five-step process for assertiveness can work just as well in practising empathy. Imagine, for instance, that Joe does not return your email inviting him to an important meeting. (Behaviour/ observation) You feel uncertain/frustrated (feeling) and you want clarity and communication (want/value/need). Can you summon your empathy to imagine what he must be feeling and wanting? Is he feeling overwhelmed and wanting some time and space to answer all his other emails? Is he feeling hesitant to answer as he would like flexibility in his future plans? When you stretch yourself to step into his shoes and imagine what he is feeling and wanting, valuing or needing, you approach the situation with curiosity versus criticism and you can express this to him. You could ring him and let him know you have not yet received a reply to your invitation and you wondered if he was feeling overwhelmed by emails or perhaps waiting to reply as he needed flexibility in his schedule. When you verbalise your questions and guess what he may be feeling and wanting, you invite an authentic dialogue. It does not matter if your empathic guess is incorrect. Usually, any sincere attempt at empathy is received and appreciated as an expression of caring and interest. Also, physiologically, empathy has been found to produce oxytocin in the recipient and so makes them more open toward you and what you have to say.[5]

Schedule a VIP appointment to work through tricky situations [6]

Ideally you would engage your own personal leadership development coach and mentor to assist you to work through your challenges as they arise. However, you may not always have that service available or accessible for a variety of reasons. You can still receive tremendous value from a self-coaching session. I call this my VIP Appointment. The VIP appointment can help you clarify your feelings, needs and ideal outcomes in regards to any given circumstance. It is a consultation you schedule with yourself to come up with a strategy or solution to deal with a challenge you are facing. As we will shortly see, identifying and understanding your feelings and needs is essential to successfully resolving challenging situations. Depending on the nature of the issue, you would ideally set aside 30 to 60 minutes for your VIP appointment.

Step 1: Get ready to take notes.

Step 2: Centre yourself with a few deep, slow breaths to begin the session.

Step 3: Set the intention to be a supportive, nonjudgmental, and kind coach to yourself for the allotted time.

Step 4: Begin the dialogue by writing the initials IC for inner coach and then your own initials in front of your response. In the following example, I use my own initials in dialogue with my inner coach.

The job of the inner coach is to listen, reflect, paraphrase, and to summarise your thoughts and feelings. Here is just the beginning of a short dialogue to give you an idea of how you could begin a VIP session between you and your own inner coach. An actual dialogue would be much longer:

IC: Good morning, Sally, what issue would you like to explore today?

SM: I'd like to look at the situation that I am facing with one of my staff.

IC: Okay, so what's the situation as you see it?

SM: John seems to be resisting our new direction, and he is not speaking up.
directly. He is just dragging his feet.

IC: Can you say more about what you mean by dragging his feet?

SM: He is behind on deadlines and not seeming to care about getting his work done.

IC: Why do you think he is behind and what makes you think he does not care?

Continue in this way with a question and answer format until you have identified all the feelings and needs of both you and the other parties involved. Conclude your self-coaching session with some action steps and acknowledge yourself for your willingness to set aside time for this vital self-reflection.

The Art of Conversation

In professional conversations, the word 'love' is rarely used, yet that is exactly what most people really want. We all want to be loved, and the feeling of love depends on mutually positive attention. This intimacy in the form of positive attention and interest is the key factor in all successful personal and business relationships. Building rapport and strengthening relationships is all about expressing your interest and caring about others. When you initiate getting to know someone, you consciously set the intention to discover their concerns as well as their passions and to hear and acknowledge them. You intentionally build a bridge of connection with them.

How do you express your love or interest specifically in a business context? The main activity of demonstrating interest involves asking sincere, open-ended questions and listening with a non-judgmental attitude. This accepting behaviour indicates your caring and encourages others to reveal more about their concerns, thoughts, and feelings. You show your continued interest and attention by asking successive questions which follow their train of thought.

Here is an example of developing and deepening a conversation using open-ended questions. An open-ended question is one which requires more than just a one word answer. It invites the other person to elaborate and tell you more. (Normally, there would be more reciprocity in a conversation, yet this sample dialogue will give you the idea of how to follow a person's train of thought).

You: So, how's it going, Paul?

Paul: Oh, not bad. . . it's been a hectic day.

You: Really? What's been happening?

Paul: I'm in the middle of a big project at work.

You: What are you working on?

Paul: We've got a new building contract for a school.

You: Interesting. What do you find most challenging about the project?

Paul: It boils down to communication. I'm coordinating a couple of teams and want to make sure everyone's focussed on the same priorities.

You: What are the main things you want them to focus on?

Paul: Firstly, we want to make sure that . . .

My brother-in-law, a former top salesperson for Hewlett Packard, taught me an important lesson about expressing interest. He told me that one of the challenges HP gave him in sales training was to see how few times he could use the word 'I' in conversation or in any correspondence. He was trained to use the word 'you' in his conversations with clients. He was also taught that the one who is asking the questions is the one with the influence. All influential communication focusses on the other party's interest. After you have demonstrated your interest in another, you will have a better chance of her or him being interested and listening to what you have to say in return. If you sincerely and consciously practice asking open-ended questions which follow another's train of thought, you develop the trust, goodwill, and warm feelings that help them to feel you care about them. Plus, as an extra benefit, you will enjoy more reciprocity in your relationships and your well-being as well as your business will benefit.

Think 'A, B, C, D, E' When Planning Presentations

How do you build this critical intimacy with people in the expanded conversation setting which we call a presentation? Remember that you will likely have a variety of different personalities in your audience, all with their own unique preferences and priorities. It is important when crafting a presentation to research your audience beforehand. The more you understand who they are and what is important to them, the stronger your connection with them will be. If you are not familiar with the audience, it is useful to apply the A B C D E technique and to build in a variety of approaches to account for each of the common communication preferences. I created the **First Five Letters System**[7] to remember the common communication preferences and behaviour types based on the numerous four-type personality profiling models such as Tetramap, Personality Plus, DISC, and

John Allesandro. The Greek physician Hippocrates was the first known person to identify these four common types which he called 'temperaments' back in the 4th century BC.[8]

Inspired to create a uniquely New Zealand-flavoured system of remembering the behaviour types, I visited the Auckland Zoo and talked to one of the staff who worked with the birds. I asked her if she knew which birds most closely aligned with the four behaviour types. I described the qualities of the four styles and she helped me decide on which bird best matched which behaviour type. I bought a puppet version of each bird at the zoo store and I now use them playfully with mentoring clients when we are looking at their habits and preferences.

Here is a guide to use when you are planning your presentation and considering the various communication styles of your audience. It will help you to reach and engage as many of your listeners as possible. Remember the first five letters of the alphabet:

A – All

We **all** have the ability to change our communication priorities and preferences, so be mindful to address all of the four common preference types:

B – Being - Kereru (Wood Pigeon)

Audience members who prioritise 'being' behaviour will tend to be more relaxed and easy listeners. They will respond to a warm and harmonious tone in your voice and presentation.

C – Checking - Ruru (Owl or Morepork)

People who display 'checking' behaviour will focus on the details of your presentation. To better engage these types, ensure you are well-organised and have your facts and figures correct.

D – Doing - Kea (New Zealand Parrot)

People in the audience who are 'doers' want you to make your point directly and quickly, so include short and practical messages to engage these people.

E – Expressing - Kākāriki (New Zealand Parakeet)

People who prefer to be more dramatically expressive, love to interact and have fun. Include plenty of action and interaction for these people. Make them the centre of attention through helping them to feel noticed and appreciated.

Think 'A, B, C, D, E' When Building Relationships

The First Five Letter System can also help you to build relationships.

Here are the common characteristics of the various human behaviour types. It is critical to develop an awareness of these universal behaviour types if you want to improve your ability to build rapport and to have positive influence. A good place to start is with understanding your own general behavioural tendencies. To better understand your own behaviour, see the description of the common behaviour types below. Just as with communication preferences, you can remember the behaviour type preferences with the first five letters of the alphabet:

A, B, C, D, E.

A - All

Remember that everyone can demonstrate ALL of the four following behaviour types depending on the situation, yet we each tend to have a dominant behaviour type pattern. The four major behaviour type preferences are characterised by four priorities:

The **Being** type wants everyone to 'get along'

The **Checking** type wants to 'get it right'

The **Doing** type wants to 'get it done'

The **Expressing** type wants to 'get attention.'

Here are some additional characteristics of the four major behaviour types. Can you spot your dominant behaviour preferences?

B – Being

Likes routine, tends to avoid change, conflict, confrontation, risk-taking, and assertiveness. Finds it hard to say 'no', and works best in a calm environment. Is loyal, friendly, a good team player and likes people to get along.

C – Checking

Likes attention to detail, accuracy and can be inflexible in following rules and logic. Instead of spontaneity, likes careful planning, quality over speed, prefers individuals to groups, is not keen on the limelight, usually thinks and reflects deliberately before acting and can be perfectionistic.

D – Doing

Is naturally competitive and achievement-oriented. Acts with authority, and prefers freedom and independence. Dominant, likes challenges, decisive and direct. Can be blunt and insensitive to others' needs.

E – Expressing

Loves being the centre of attention – optimistic, enthusiastic, not too good with detail or time management. Can be superficial, likes variety and is a great networker. Likes informal style, is creative, can be impulsive, loves change and spontaneous self-expression.

Reflect on your own behaviour style. Which style describes your typical way of acting most closely? Or, are you well-balanced and flexible in changing styles depending on the situation? It is common for partners to display complementary behaviour types to balance out the needs of the relationship. For example, I tend to lean more towards the doing and expressing behaviours and my partner generally prefers the being and checking behaviours. I have wanted to finish this book quickly, to get it done, and he has been urging me to slow down and take my time to get it right. Together, my desire to keep moving and to get the book finished combined with his desire to make sure it is well-written and accurate makes us a better team. However, this means we need to embrace the natural tension that arises when I want to move fast and he wants to move more slowly (pace tension).

The other tension that can arise happens when one person is more people-focussed and the other is more task-focussed (priority tension). I recently encountered this tension at a meeting with a prospective client. I wanted to get to know him, to explore our mutual connections and to build rapport at the start of our meeting. I also wanted to explore possible ways of working together. Within what seemed like a few seconds of my asking him where he was from, he abruptly changed the course of the conversation. "Can we please *focus* and talk about what we are looking for from you?' he asked me. I was stopped in my tracks. I promptly changed gear from my people-oriented behaviour and realised I was dealing with a task-oriented behaviour. He wanted to get down to business right away. Although I initially felt hurt that he did not seem interested in social interaction, my understanding of the four behaviour types prevented me from taking his comment personally. I knew this was merely a matter of priority tension.

Pace and priority tensions can cause conflict or serve to enrich the outcomes of a particular relationship or team. As long as you view the behaviour types with awareness and veneration for the gifts that each type brings, the differences can be a source of creativity and resourcefulness in relationships and teams. The key to veneration is embracing all the behaviour types and treating yourself and others with a respectful and appreciative attitude.

I wish for you a heart full of veneration for the wide diversity of people you will encounter during your life and work. Veneration is a capacity you can continually develop and probably the most difficult of the six keys outlined in this book. It is easier to say 'accept yourself and others' than to fully do that. It is interesting that the Christian Church refers to veneration as the act of honouring saints. The word 'veneration' is derived from the latin verb *venerare*, meaning to regard with reverence and respect. Veneration refers to the high regard one has for someone's greatness or value. May you learn to venerate yourself and others, carrying the quality of deep respect with you as you step out into the world and express your 'voice of leadership'.

Key # 6 Summary:

✓ Veneration begins with self-compassion

✓ Assertiveness is a life or death matter

✓ Strengthen feelings and needs literacy for successful communication

✓ The art of conversation depends on expressing interest in others

✓ A-B-C-D-E helps you remember the different behaviour types

Conclusion and Next Steps

You now have a greater awareness of the six keys to presence, influence, and creative confidence. It is time to think about how you will incorporate your new insights into your life. What new habits do you want to adopt? What old habits do you want to release? How has your vision for yourself and your work changed? What project are you ready to start or what project are you ready to finish? Which relationships do you want to strengthen and which relationships do you want to let go? Below are some questions to help you integrate what you have learned about the six keys of voice, vision, values, vitality, visibility, and veneration.

Reflections and Next Steps Exercise:

1. What are the three top insights or benefits you experienced through reading this book and then engaging with the exercises?

_____

_____

_____

_____

_____

2. How would you summarise the essence of what you have learned?

_____

_____

_____

_____

_____

3. What will you keep doing?

_____

_____

_____

_____

4. What will you stop doing?

_____

_____

_____

_____

_____

5. What will you start doing?

_____

_____

_____

_____

_____

6. What support will you put in place for yourself to keep moving forward?

_____

_____

_____

_____

_____

E tī! E tā! E tū[11]
Strike Your own note
Do it with passion
Stand tall and strong

It can be helpful to engage with others who are on the same journey of strengthening their voice of leadership. For this reason, I offer online and in person, group and individual mentoring programs to assist you in your professional development.

Together, we can work through the exercises in this book, in person or online, and you can gain valuable support from your peers who are also on a similar journey. If you would like to explore this possibility, you can contact me through my website, www.sallymabelle.com

Appendix

Psychological
and Emotional Health
Self-Assessment[1]

This self-assessment runs across two pages from left to right.

SELF-AWARENESS	LITTLE OR NO AWARENESS OF THOUGHTS, FEELINGS, BEHAVIOURS
SELF-TRUST	HIGH RELIANCE ON EXTERNAL AUTHORITY FOR GUIDANCE
RATIONALITY	IRRATIONAL, CATASTROPHIC THINKING REGARDING LIFE/ RELATIONSHIPS
ACCOUNTABILTY	BLAMES OTHERS, HIGHLY REACTIVE, AVOIDS RESPONSIBILITY
SENSE OF PURPOSE	UNDIRECTED, APATHETIC, LACKS VISION, UNDISCIPLINED
SENSE OF MORALITY	LYING, CHEATING, DECEIVING SELF AND OTHERS, TAKING SHORTCUTS
BELONGING	ISOLATED, LONELY, LACKING CLOSE RELATIONSHIPS
SELF-NURTURING BEHAVIOUR	POOR NUTRITION, NO EXERCISE, SEDENTARY, NEGATIVE FOCUS, CRITICAL OF SELF AND OTHERS
SENSE OF HUMOUR	SERIOUS, SOMBER, RARELY SMILES, LAUGHS, SELF-ABSORBED IN PROBLEMS
ATTITUDE OF GRATITUDE	FEELS SLIGHTED, RESENTFUL, LACK, CRITICAL OF CURRENT LIFE SITUATION
GIVING AND RECEIVING	PROTECTIVE OR 'TIGHT' WITH MONEY, TIME, LOVE, FEELS LACK, NEVER ENOUGH, DIFFICULTY IN RECEIVING AND GIVING AFFECTION/PRAISE
FORGIVENESS	HOLDS GRUDGES, ANGER, BLAME, BLAMING, JUDGES SELF AND OTHERS HARSHLY
FLEXIBILITY/OPEN-MINDEDNESS	RIGID IN PATTERNS OF THINKING/BEHAVING, UNCOMPROMISING, ONLY SEES OWN POINT OF VIEW

Reflect on each of the mental health indicators below and assess your current level on a scale from 1-5.

1 2 3 4 5	HIGH AWARENESS OF THOUGHTS, FEELINGS, BEHAVIOURS
1 2 3 4 5	RELIANCE ON INNER GUIDANCE PROMINENT
1 2 3 4 5	RATIONAL, LOGICAL, PRACTICAL THINKING
1 2 3 4 5	ACKNOWLEDGES OWN POWER TO CREATE INTERNAL STATE, ACCEPTING RESPONSIBILITY
1 2 3 4 5	FOCUSSED, ENTHUSIASTIC, VISION-ORIENTED, DISCIPLINED
1 2 3 4 5	SEEKS TO DO NO HARM - SEEKS TO SERVE OTHERS WITH ONE'S GIFTS AND TALENTS
1 2 3 4 5	FULLY INVOLVED IN CLOSE RELATIONSHIPS, FAMILY, COMMUNITY, INTERDEPENDENT
1 2 3 4 5	ADEQUATE SLEEP, PROPER NUTRITION, REGULAR EXERCISE AND RELAXATION, POSITIVE FOCUS, SELF-ACCEPTING
1 2 3 4 5	LIGHT, SMILES AND LAUGHS OFTEN, HAS PERSPECTIVE /OBJECTIVITY ON HIS/HER ISSUES
1 2 3 4 5	FEELS GRATEFUL FOR MANY BLESSINGS, APPRECIATES SELF AND OTHERS, FEELS ABUNDANCE, ENJOYS CURRENT LIFE SITUATION
1 2 3 4 5	FREELY ACCEPTS AND GIVES AFFECTION/PRAISE, EXPERIENCES ABUNDANCE OF GIFTS: TIME, LOVE, MONEY
1 2 3 4 5	EMPATHETIC/ COMPASSIONATE/ LETS GO EASILY OF ANGER/ BLAME, ACCEPTS SELF AND OTHERS
1 2 3 4 5	OPEN-MINDED, WILLING TO COMPROMISE, ACCEPTS OTHERS POINTS OF VIEW AS VALID

Appendix

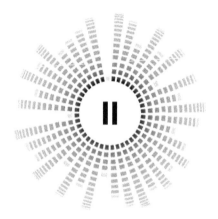

Common Feelings List[1]

Common Feelings List

MAD	indifferent	GLAD	AFRAID
aggravated	nauseous	absorbed	alarmed
annoyed	off centre	alive	anxious
bitter	tired	appreciative	concerned
bored	ungrounded	awed	conflicted
bothered	weary	comfortable	desperate
cynical		confident	disturbed
exasperated	**SAD**	content	doubtful
furious	blue	eager	frozen
frustrated	depressed	enthusiastic	guarded
impatient	disappointed	grateful	hesitant
indignant	discouraged	happy	insecure
peeved	doubtful	keen	nervous
perturbed	down	open	numb
pessimistic	empty	passionate	overwhelmed
worked up	grieving	peaceful	panicked
	gutted	positive	powerless
BAD	heavy	satisfied	puzzled
ashamed	hurt	secure social	reluctant
embarrassed	lonely	trusting	
guilty			

Common Feelings List Notes

This list is a small sampling of feeling words to increase your emotional awareness and ability to communicate. If what you are feeling does not seem to fit under one of the five categories (Mad, Bad, Sad, Glad, or Afraid), it may be a combination of feelings, such as mad and sad when you feel embarrassed.

Pay attention to physical sensations such as a tightness in your jaw or neck, a rush of heat in your face, a constriction in your throat or stomach, or an expansive feeling in your chest. These are your signals to alert you to your nonverbal feeling states.

Appendix

Common Needs List[1]

Common Needs List

VENERATION
Acceptance
Acknowledgement
Appreciation
Consideration
Dignity
Empathy
Encouragement
Eye contact
Equality
Fairness
Flexibility
Forgiveness
Goodwill
Respect

VISIBILITY
Community
Connection
Contribution
Closeness
Inclusion
Interest
Mutuality
Reciprocity
Support
Transparency
Understanding
Validation

VITALITY
Air, Food, Water
Balance
Beauty
Comfort/Ease
Exercise

Harmony
Inspiration
Meaning
Movement
Order
Peace
Purpose
Quiet/Silence
Rest
Safety
Solitude
Space
Time

**VOICE AND
SELF-EXPRESSION**
Adventure
Challenge
Choice
Creativity
Discipline
Experience
Freedom
Individuality
Mastery
Play/Fun/Laughter
Reflection
Self-direction
Self-worth

ACCOUNTABILITY
Accepting limits
Clarity
Consistency
Data

Decision-making
Discernment
Honesty
Humility
Information
Integrity
Learning
Neutrality
Patience
Progress
Punctuality

**CELEBRATING
BEGINNINGS**
Acknowledgements
Ceremony, Ritual
Delight
Enjoyment
Humour
Welcomes

**HONOURING
ENDINGS**
Acknowledging
Achievements
Acknowledging Regrets
Celebrating Wins
Celebrating Dreams
Fulfilled
Grieving Dreams
Unfulfilled
Grieving Losses
Healing
Mourning Lost
Relationships

173

Notes

Acknowledgements

1. Ngā mihi is the indigenous Maori phrase for acknowledgements and thanks – as I have lived here in Aotearoa, New Zealand for the past 14 years, I have come to prefer this phrase over the traditional 'thank you.'

Preface

1. Pepeha guidance by Atutahi Riki, kaumatua (tribal elder) of Waikato, Tainui Waka.

Introduction

1. Dweck, C. *(2008)*. *Mindset.* New York, NY: Ballantine Books.

Key #1 Voice

1. Covey, S. R. (1990). *The 7 Habits of Highly Effective People.* New York, NY: Simon and Schuster.
2. Covey, S. R. (2005). *The Eighth Habit.* New York, NY: Simon and Schuster.
3. Brown, B. (2012). *Daring Greatly: How the Courage to Be Vulnerable Transforms the Way We Live, Love, Parent, and Lead.* New York, NY: Penguin Putnam.
4. Johns Hopkins Medicine, www.hopkinsmedicine.org, Baltimore, MD, USA.

5. Flax, R. (September 1990). The American Salesman Magazine, p. 13, Burlington, Iowa.
6. Croston, G. (29th November 2012). The Real Story of Risk, Psychology Today, psychologytoday.com blog
7. Zandan, N. CEO and Co-founder Quantified Communications, (5 October, 2016). *Why Do We Fear Public Speaking?* www.quantifiedcommunications.com/blog/why-do-we-fear-public-speaking
8. From the movie, *Singin' in the Rain*, 1952, Metro-Goldwyn-Mayer.
9. Ko, S. J. (20th November, 2014). Psychological Science Journal, 20th November, San Diego State University (SDSU), and her colleagues Drs. M. Sadler (SDSU) and A. Galinsky (of Columbia University).
10. Oliver, M. (1986). 'The Journey.' A poem published in Dreamwork. New York, NY: Atlantic Monthly Press.
11. Whyte, D. (1990) *Where Many Rivers Meet,* Kingston, WA: Many Rivers Press.

Key #2 Vision

1. Hall, V. (2009). *The Truth about Trust in Business.* Austin, TX: Emerald Book Company.
2. Dobrowolski, P. (4th January, 2013 TED talk). Strategic Illustration.
3. Dale E. 1969. Cone of experience, Educational Media: Theory into Practice. Wiman RV (ed)., Columbus, Ohio: Charles Merrill
4. Bolte Taylor, J. (2008). TED, My Stroke of Insight, youtube video.
5. Lewis, N. (2011). *The Interpretation of Dreams and Portents in Antiquity.* Mundelein, IL: Bolchazy-Carducci Publishers.
6. Castor, H. (2015). *Joan of Arc.* London, England: Faber and Faber.

Key #3 Values

1. Winners are chosen via a survey of both employees and employers, conducted by Crain's New York Business Magazine in partnership with Best Companies Group, a research organisation whose mission is to "identify and recognize" places of employment that are leading the way in defining the employee experience of the 21st century.
2. Patel, S. (2015). 10 Examples of Companies with Fantastic Cultures. Entrepreneur Magazine (6 August, 2015), Irvine, California.
3. Ludema, J. and Johnson, A. (2014). Making Values Meaningful: A Menu of Options for Senior Leaders. Chicago, Il: Benedictine University. http://cvdl.ben.edu
4. Spiller, C., Barclay-Kerr, H., and Panoho, J. (2015). *Wayfinding Leadership: Ground-breaking Wisdom for Developing Leaders.* Wellington, New Zealand: Huia Publishing.
5. Lally, P. (2009). How are Habits Formed: Modelling Habit Formation in the Real World. European Journal of Social Psychology, (40)6.

Key #4 Vitality

1. University of California's Edx (2015). 'Science of Happiness' course, Week 8, 'Gratitude.'
2. Nair, S., Sagar M., Sollers J 3rd, Consedine N., Broadbent E., of the Department of Psychological Medicine and Bioengineering Institute, The University of Auckland, *Do slumped and upright postures affect stress responses? A randomized trial.* Health Psychology (2015) Jun:34(6) 632-41.
3. Mabelle, S. (10th May, 2015), Collaboritude: The Four Foundations for Collaboration and Innovation, Blog. www.sallymabelle.com/blog/2016/5/10/collaboritude
4. Csíkszentmihályi, M. (2008). *Flow: The Psychology of Optimal Experience.* New York, NY: Harper Collins.

5. Bert VanDijk inspired me to add 'intuition' to my list of senses in his Presence workshop 2015, toiora.com
6. 'Science of Happiness' Edx Course (2009) Berkeley, California, University of California.
7. Page-Gould, E. Associate Professor at the University of Toronto, Department of Psychology (Social/Personality/ Abnormal Area)

Key #5 Visibility

1. Australian Thought Leader, Matt Church, taught me these memorable phrases: 'Why This, Why Now, Why Me.' www. mattchurch.com

Key #6 Veneration

1. Neff, K. (2011). *Self-Compassion: The Proven Power of Being Kind to Yourself.* New York, NY: William Morrow.
2. Rosenberg, M. (2003). *Nonviolent Communication: A Language of Life.* Encinitas, CA: PuddleDancer Press.
3. Gladwell, M. (2008) *Outliers: The Story of Success,* Boston, MA: Little, Brown and Company
4. Spiller, C., Barclay-Kerr, H., and Panoho, J. (2015). *Wayfinding Leadership: Ground-breaking Wisdom for Developing Leaders.* Wellington, New Zealand: Huia Publishing.
5. Barraza, J. A. PhD. (2010). The Physiology of Empathy: Linking Oxytocin to Empathic Responding. Claremont, CA: Claremont Graduate University.
6. University of Santa Monica, 'Spiritual Psychology' programme, adapted from self-counseling technique.
7. Mabelle, S. (10th May, 2015), Collaboritude:The Four Foundations for Collaboration and Innovation, Blog. http:// www.sallymabelle. com/blog/2016/5/10/collaboritude
8. Rolfe, R. (2002). *The Four Temperaments: A Rediscovery of the Ancient Way of Understanding Health and Character.* New York, NY: Marlowe and Company.

Conclusion and Next Steps

1. Expression as taught by Shafia Mariam Stevens of Ngāi Tahu ancestry in her dance of universal peace inspired by the Māori tradition.

Appendix I - Psychological and Emotional Health Self- Assessment

1. Mabelle, S. (20 April, 1990) Loving In Action: My Current Theory of Counselling, written as part of University of Santa Monica's Spiritual Psychology programme.
This is not intended to replace professional assessment and advice for serious mental health concerns.

Appendix II - Common Feelings List

1. This feelings list was inspired by Philadelphia-based acting teacher Gordon Phillips, the New Zealand Ministry of Education's Hauora Health Curriculum, and the work of Nonviolent Communication by Dr. Marshall B. Rosenberg and the Center for Nonviolent Communication.

Appendix III - Common Needs List

1. This needs list is based on the work of Dr. Marshall B. Rosenberg and the Center for Nonviolent Communication and Marie R. Miyashiro's Needs Inventory for the Workplace in her book The Empathy Factor: Both publications available through Puddle Dancer Press, www. cnvc.org.

About the Author

Sally Mabelle, M.Ed, B.A. (Rhetoric and Communication), has spent the last 25+ years developing the 'Voice of Leadership' method of developing positive presence and influence. Combining her professional background in Communication, Education, Psychology, and Acting, she now promotes and teaches the essential leadership skills of voice projection, emotional connection, and mindful presence to help people step up and show up to make a powerful difference for themselves, their teams, and their organisations.

Sally has worked with senior executives in Aotearoa New Zealand and the U.S.A. from sectors such as banking, insurance, accounting, healthcare, IT, and other professional service organisations. She has also worked with not-for-profit organisations and various schools in the Tāmaki Makaurau/Auckland area. She started out her career as a project manager for a software company in Silicon Valley, working also in customer service and sales before launching out on her own.

Sally currently works as an individual and group mentor and coach for leaders and those aspiring to leadership. Her primary areas of expertise are in leadership communication, presentation, vocal empowerment, assertiveness, conflict resolution, creative confidence, and collaboration.

Work with Sally Mabelle:

To enquire about online or in person group and individual mentoring programmes or Sally's keynote presentations, you can contact her through her website at www.sallymabelle.com

Lightning Source UK Ltd.
Milton Keynes UK
UKHW021127031120
372721UK00009B/1999